Pyzdek's Guide to SPC
Volume one: Fundamentals

Thomas Pyzdek

Quality Consultant

Published by:

ASQC-Quality Press *Milwaukee, Wisconsin*
Quality Publishing, Inc. *Tucson, Arizona*

Pyzdek, Thomas
 Pyzdek's Guide to SPC: Vol. 1, Fundamentals
 (Pyzdek's Guide to SPC; Vol. 1)
 1.   Quality control. I. Title. II. Series: Pyzdek's Guide to SPC; v. 1.
Library of Congress Catalog Card Number: 89-92170
ISBN 0-930011-03-1

Quality Publishing, Inc.
2405 N Avenida Sorgo, Tucson, Arizona 85749-9305

Current printing (last digit)
10 9 8 7

Preface

The decades that have passed since Dr. Walter A. Shewhart introduced the concepts of Statistical Process Control (SPC) have not diminished their popularity. In fact, these simple but powerful methods of improving productivity and quality are more popular now than ever before. There is a good reason for this: SPC works.

However, before SPC can be effectively used it must be understood. This book is based on an SPC seminar that provided training to thousands of people over a period of years. The author used SPC methods to evaluate the effectiveness of the materials. Since the "students" were actually paying customers, they were not afraid to voice their true feelings regarding the shortcomings of the book–or the instructor. This crucible of honesty resulted in a large number of changes to the materials and, I believe, a much better book.

One of the difficulties encountered over and over again was a wide range of needs and backgrounds among the students. This presented a number of problems when preparing the subject matter. When advanced material was covered many students were confused. When basics were discussed many students were bored. This experience lead to the creation of a series with three separate volumes instead of a single book. The subject matter is divided into Fundamentals, Special Applications, and Advanced Techniques. Workbooks and instructor's guides are available for each volume. Volume one is available now, the other two volumes are being prepared and will be released at a future date.

The first volume, Fundamentals, provides material that everyone must know. Most people will not need to go beyond this volume. Volume One is intended for all levels employees in the organization, from the engineer to the machine operator, from top managment to the hourly worker. It provides an introduction to SPC, as well as information on how SPC is effectively managed and implemented.

Volume two, Applications and Special Techniques, is designed for the SPC coordinator, quality analyst, or engineer responsible for designing products, processes, or quality programs. It discusses special topics and applications of SPC such as short runs, CuSum charts, process capability analysis, SPC for automated manufacturing, SPC for continuous processes, etc.. The emphasis is on applications.

Volume three is intended for use by the experienced SPC coordinator or quality engineer concerned with the correct application of SPC in a wide variety of real world situations. The emphasis is on "special case situations" that seem to arise with disturbing regularity as the SPC program is implemented. Volume three discusses the effect of failing to meet the assumptions of SPC. In some cases, exact solutions are presented. Non-parametric methods of SPC are offered for dealing with data whose distribution may not be known. Process capability analysis using emperical distributions is discussed. Other subjects covered include the effects of measurement error on control limits, statistical tolerancing, economic models for control charts, methods of updating control limits, etc..

Table of Contents

Pyzdek's Guide to SPC
Volume one : Fundamentals

CHAPTER 1

INTRODUCTION TO SPC

Objectives

After completing this section you will:

- Understand the importance of quality to your company and to America.
- Understand the importance of management's role in quality improvement.
- Know the features all successful SPC programs share.

Quality as a business strategy

Quality has become a hot issue. In fact, you could say that quality has evolved beyond a mere issue. Quality has become *the* business strategy of the 80's and 90's. There is one reason that goes farther than any other toward explaining this: Japan. Since 1950 Japan's economy has grown steadily, taking market share from other world economies. The nation to lose the most to Japan, in terms of market share, has been the United States. The mix of products that have been subjected to Japan's onslaught include many industries. Smokestack industries like automobiles and steel have been the subject of much press. But hardly anyone noticed that Japan also produces far more of many other products than their United States competitors, and that their lead is increasing. Hardly anyone, that is, except the American workers who lost their jobs to the Japanese.

Until recently, America's response to this has been to impose import restrictions and to claim unfair Japanese advantage due to a variety of mistaken reasons. As one business observer noted, the most used part of the corporate anatomy has been the pointing finger. We've seen our workers accused of being lazier than their Japanese counterparts. We are told that the workers in America are overpaid, causing our products to cost too much. We are told that it is "Japan Inc.", a consortium of government, industry,

1

academic, and banking powers working together to pick off target products. Hardly a week goes by without some American business group or another standing up in front of congress pleading for protection.

Strangely, all of this was predicted in 1950 by an American, Dr. W. Edwards Deming. The story began right after World War II. The United States was determined to avoid the mistakes made after World War I. The goal was nothing less than to rebuild the war shattered economy of the world, including the economies of America's wartime enemies. Europe was to be rebuilt under the Marshall Plan. Japan was to be handled differently. Japan presented the planners with special problems. A tiny island nation, Japan has few natural resources. She is isolated from the key markets of North America and Europe. Worst of all, in the post war era, Japan had a reputation as the supplier of cheap junk! The United States realized that if they were to make any progress at all, Japan's quality reputation had to change dramatically.

Modern quality control was literally invented in the United States by Dr. Walter A. Shewhart of Bell Laboratories. It is fair to say that the techniques of modern quality control were vital in our war effort. During the war the use of these methods had become widespread throughout industry and the post war era in America was one of enthusiasm for "statistical quality control." Dozens of articles appeared in the business press extolling the virtues of this new technology. Even the popular press was getting on the bandwagon. Thus it was only natural to call in quality control experts from the United States to help Japan with her serious quality problems. One of the experts called upon was Dr. W Edwards Deming. Deming had also been giving lectures on quality in America. In America he addressed engineers and specialists, in Japan he addressed *top management.* Deming found the Japanese eager students, CEO's of major Japanese companies took Deming's teachings out into their factories and applied them firsthand. They returned with their charts and data filled with excitement about what they'd learned. The Japanese industrial revolution had begun.

Japan no longer has a reputation for shoddy quality. Far from it, "Made in Japan" now *means* top quality. Figure 1.1 is from Dr. Joseph M. Juran, a leading expert on quality and another visitor to Japan in the immediate postwar years.

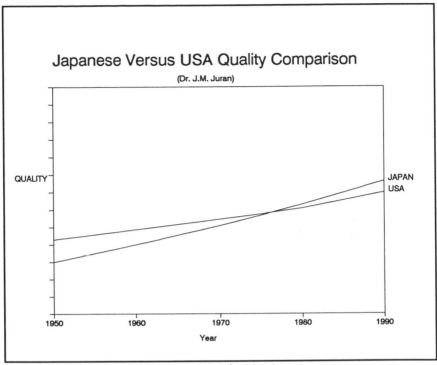

Figure 1.1 - Dr. Juran's Estimates of USA Vs. Japan

As Japan practiced "hands-on management," using modern statistical tools to evaluate their products and their customer's expectations, American management moved toward increasing specialization. The American top management philosophy was to "let the quality experts handle it." Under the American system the customer and his expectations was under the jurisdiction of the marketing group, quality was the responsibility of the quality control department, etc. By 1980 the CEO and COO had effectively withdrawn from day-to-day operations. When the American Society for Quality Control (ASQC) surveyed chief executives on the quality of their company's products they found that *nearly 2 out of 3 felt that they didn't know enough about their products to answer the questions*. Those who did answer the survey questions were found to be at odds with their customers, as figure 1.2 demonstrates. Dr. Deming places responsibility for quality improvement squarely on the shoulders of top-management. In fact, the Deming philosophy has been em-

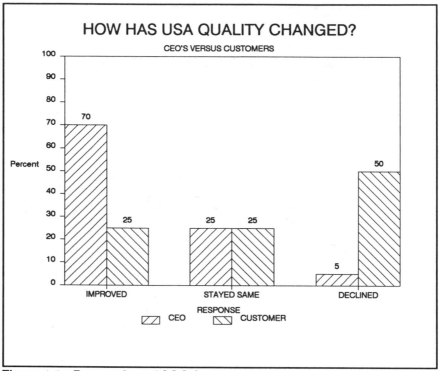

Figure 1.2 - Percent from ASQC Survey

bodied in a set of principles known collectively as Deming's 14 points for management. These points have been grouped into categories by one of America's leading auto makers, and they are presented in figure 1.3. Besides Deming, there are several other venerable quality consultants whose influence on quality has been profound. These gentlemen are sometimes called the "gurus of quality." The approaches taken by the gurus vary. Philip Crosby bases his quality philosophy on zero defects as a performance standard. The program must be personally directed by top management since it is they who set the standards for the entire company. Improvement is measured by the cost of quality, which is the cost of doing things wrong. Quality is defined as conformance to requirements. The method of achieving quality improvement is prevention. These concepts are formalized into the "4 absolutes of quality" shown in table 1.1.

Table 1.1–Crosby's Absolutes of Quality

Item	Definition
Definition of quality	Quality is defined as conformance to requirements
System for obtaining quality	Prevention
Performance standard	Zero defects
Quality measurement	Cost of (non) quality

Another of the gurus was mentioned previously, Dr. J. M. Juran. Juran's approach, as that of all the gurus, stresses the importance of top management leadership. Quality is defined as fitness for use. The improvement process becomes institutionalized in the Juran system, with personnel being organized into teams and trained in the use of important diagnostic tools. Juran originated the term "Pareto analysis."

One of Japan's contributions to the population of gurus is Dr. Kaoru Ishikawa. The Ishikawa program is called "Total Quality Control," a term first coined by still another America quality guru, Armand Feigenbaum. Ishikawa's interpretation of total quality control incorporates various elements of Japanese culture in addition to the basic quality systems. Ishikawa is the inventor of the cause and effect diagram, also called the Ishikawa diagram.

While the gurus are adamant that their philosophies must be implemented in pure form, most companies "mix and match" according to their individual needs.

Program planning and organization

By now America has had considerable experience with quality improvement. Some of these programs are failing while others are enjoying success. Although America is still in the learning process there are some clear lessons which have already been learned. These lessons can be condensed into features that all of the successful programs share.

Management Principles

1. Innovate and allocate resources to fulfill the long-range needs of the company and customer rather than short-term profitability.

2. Discard the old philosophy of accepting defective products.

8. Reduce fear throughout the organization by encouraging open, two-way, non-punitive communication. The economic loss resulting from fear to ask questions or report trouble is appalling.

9. Help reduce waste by encouraging design, research and sales people to learn more about the problems of production.

14. Make maximum use of statistical knowledge and talent in your company.

Training

6. Institute more thorough, better job-related training.

7. Provide supervision with knowledge of statistical methods; encourage use of these methods to identify which defects should be investigated for solution.

12. Institute rudimentary statistical training on a broad scale.

13. Institute a vigorous program for retraining people in new skills to keep up with changes in materials, methods, product designs, and machinery.

Implementation Concepts

3. Eliminate dependence on mass inspection for quality control; instead, depend on process control through statistical techniques.

5. Use statistical techniques to identify the two sources of waste - system (94%) and local faults (6%); strive to constantly reduce this waste.

10. Eliminate the use of goals and slogans to encourage productivity, unless training and management support are also provided.

11. Closely examine the impact of work standards. Do they consider quality or help anyone do a better job?

Suppliers

4. Reduce the number of multiple source suppliers. Price has no meaning without integral consideration for quality. Encourage suppliers to use statistical process control.

Figure 1.3 - Deming's 14 Points

FEATURE 1 - TOP MANAGEMENT LEADERSHIP

To the best of my knowledge, there has never been a successful program for long-term quality or productivity improvement that did not have the active support and involvement of top management of the company. This support is embodied in a variety of ways, all of which transcend mere "moral support." In the most successful programs the support manifests itself by the active involvement of the Chief Executive Officer (CEO) at every stage of the program.

The top-management in the successful company get training in the concepts of total quality control. The extent of this training varies widely, ranging from 4 hours to 5 days of initial training. Regardless of the amount of training, top management of the companies with successful quality improvement programs "get religion" and firmly believes that the program will be successful. I've been told that if you must choose between understanding and believing, take belief. The successful companies seem to bear this out.

It may be important at this point to discuss just how management can reach the large number of people it must reach to create the proper atmosphere. The importance of the proper atmosphere can not be over stated and creating it is top-management's primary task. Management reaches its people by their example. People do as they see their leaders do. And the word is spread throughout the company like wildfire through storytelling.

As a consultant I must be able to walk into a company and get an immediate feel for the type of company I am dealing with; this skill is essential to my livelihood. Over the years I've dealt with dozens of companies and I have had the opportunity to subject my first impressions to the test of time. Based on this I feel confident in saying that, usually, I can accurately determine the type of company I am dealing within just a few hours. My method is very simple: I listen to the stories people tell. Listen...

The management of the company bragged to me about how well they treated their workers and how close they were to their workers. Still I sensed resentment from the workers themselves. As I worked in the office next door I heard the new supervisor tell his workers "I don't have a bird dog, I don't have a boat, and I don't have a new jeep." This was greeted with wild laughter and applause. The supervisor continued to say that he would provide whatever help he could to the people. I was later told that the top management of the plant was a group of "good ol' boys" that chummed around together, often sneaking out of the plant at 1 p.m. for golf, fishing, or whatever. It seems that over the years the plant manager had acquired a bird-dog, a boat, and a jeep. His cronies each did the same just afterward.

Having listened to the story and the response it received, what do you think the employee's response would be to the introduction of a quality improvement program by plant management? Here's another true story:

The workers were gathered about looking at a group of microcircuit substrates that one of them held in her hand. Being a quality improvement consultant I was naturally interested when I heard that the discussion was the possibility of defects. "Should we clean the stacker?" one of the workers asked. Another answered, "after Sam's last visit out here, what do you think?" They laughed, and cleaned the stacker. It seems that Sam, the plant manager, had been wandering around the area and happened upon two people discussing a batch of defective parts. They were arguing over how big a pit a part must have before it would be called a defective. Sam answered the question for them, "if there's a pit, it's defective!"

Stories are the mechanism used to transmit the culture of a nation or of a company. Storytelling was used for millennia to pass history from generation to generation. What are your company's stories about? It's what your company is about, too. Listen carefully and you will know if your new program is succeeding or failing. Is the talk of new stories? When a difficult order is shipped on time are the stories about the excitement of meeting a difficult challenge, or of unfair customer demands grudgingly met? Is the new SPC program talked about by comparing it to past failures, or is the story associated with the new program about the boss showing up unexpectedly to personally check on an important quality detail? The answers will tell you all you need to know to predict success or failure.

FEATURE 2 - TEAMWORK

The successful programs all make use of teams. The American system has encouraged functional specialization while simultaneously evaluating performance based on short-term goals. This combination has lead to quasi-autonomous departments that are internally optimized but whose behavior is detrimental to the company as a whole. The management-appointed, interdepartmental team appears to be a response to the need for holistic perspectives.

Let me clear up the meaning with a couple of examples from my own experience.

> *Company X was in the aerospace business and the company's on-line computer network was its nerve center. Literally everything the company did was tied in with the computer system in one way or another. Order entry, inventory control, payroll, and a host of other vital activities were "on-line." This being the case, management became concerned when the volume of activity reached a level that began to have an adverse impact on response time at the computer terminals, the window to the computer. It didn't take long for management to approve the installation of a modern new system that promised relief.*

A few months after the new system was installed I found myself working with a quality control circle composed of clerical personnel. Oddly, the circle was working on the problem of response time at their computer data entry terminals. Their study revealed that the software provided with the new system had been rewritten by the data processing department to give priority to data processing jobs. While this was obviously great for data processing it was unquestionably bad news for the company as a whole!

> *"This year's top priority is to reduce scrap, rework, and warranty" the division manager announced. A member of the staff asked for a review of the previous year's goals and whether they had been achieved. Last year's top goal: reduce the percentage of the sales dollar spent on purchased materials. The goal had been met, in fact exceeded, by a considerable margin. After the meeting I was told by the managers of manufacturing, engineering, and quality control that the reason this year's goals were scrap, rework, and warranty expenditures was that last year's goals were met by buying the cheapest available materials regardless of quality.*

While teams are not a panacea for short-sighted management, they do provide a forum for expressing different points of view. By setting up a direct line of reporting to top management the holistic perspective is reinforced. It is a lot harder to pass the buck when the person to whom it is being passed is sitting next to you.

The teams are given charters by management. They are trained in problem solving skills and are expected to meet regularly. Their progress and problems are monitored by top management and top management participates in the team projects. The entire SPC program is based on the team approach.

FEATURE 3 - STATISTICAL METHODS

The use of statistical methods provides a dimension that can not be obtained in any other way. Statistical evaluation of data immediately shifts the attention to *facts* and away from opinions and personalities. Statistical methods will also help you determine whether improvement will require action on the system or action within the system. Without statistical evaluation the action you take will often be inappropriate and it may even aggravate the problem you are trying to solve. A very important part of the SPC training is to teach you to use statistical methods in your problem solving efforts.

FEATURE 4 - COMPREHENSIVE TRAINING

The successful companies are obsessed with training. This obsession is wise: poor training is the root cause of many quality problems. Training includes job related training, training in basic statistical methods and concepts, and even training in basic skills such as reading and mathematics.
Training emphasis is one of the major differences between Japanese and American companies. One evening, the day before I was to call on a client who was implementing a quality improvement program, I watched a special program on the Public Broadcasting System. The special was about Japanese culture. It also discussed Japanese businesses. One of the items that impressed me was that Japan had retained the apprenticeship system. A lens polisher at Nikon, for example, serves a three year apprenticeship before he is allowed to polish lenses on his own. The next day I visited my client, a company that manufactures ceramic substrates that are used in electronic hybrid microcircuits. As we evaluated a control chart it became clear that the manufacturer was having trouble because the process setup was not being properly done. In fact, the losses from setup were running between 8% and 20% of the total production quantity. The engineer was puzzled because the setup should have been quite simple, a matter of only three settings. When

we checked we discovered that the person doing the setup had *received no training at all*!

FEATURE 5 - SUPPLIER INVOLVEMENT

In the successful companies there is a tendency to have a smaller number of suppliers, especially for key parts. The suppliers are involved much earlier, perhaps even in the product design phase. Efforts are made to get "families" of parts to the same supplier so that he can provide better input into the design process. In other words, the supplier is given contracts for groups of related parts so he can better understand how they work together.

The supplier's *process* becomes a concern. No longer do the successful companies accept the "parts meet spec." attitude. The use of mass sorting to separate bad parts from good is viewed as a stop-gap only; the goal is a supplier process in statistical control. Often the customer provides statistical training and consulting to the smaller supplier company.

Communication between supplier and customer continues after the parts are delivered. Suppliers are brought to the customer's plant to observe the use of their parts and to help solve problems. In short, a two-way communication is established at a very early stage and continued through the entire process of production and final delivery.

Obviously, the SPC program is based on intense supplier-customer cooperation and communication. This closer working relationship can not help but improve understanding between customer and supplier. This will in turn provide a basis for improved quality.

FEATURE 6 - CUSTOMIZED PROGRAMS

No two successful companies have the same program. Even though they share the similarities mentioned in Features 1 through 5, every program has its own unique features, usually designed by top management. The programs reflect the culture of the company; e.g. some are very formal, others very loosely organized. Some programs are adapted to the customer being served, such as programs that sell to the military. The point is that *you* must develop your own program, there is no such thing as an "off-the-rack quality program." It is your job, and that of your management, to find a way to incorporate the best of these ideas into your own unique program.

CHAPTER 2

WORKING IN GROUPS

Objectives

After completing this section you will:

- Understand the group process.
- Know why the group process is important in SPC
- Know how to work toward consensus in a group setting.

Groups and SPC

There are two ways to make improvements with SPC: improve performance given the current system, or improve the system itself. Most of the time improving performance given the current system can be accomplished by individuals working alone. For example, an operator might make certain adjustments to his machine. Studies indicate that this sort of action will be responsible for about 15% of the improvements. The remaining 85% of all improvements will require changing the system itself. This is almost never accomplished by individuals working alone. It requires group action. Thus, the vast majority of SPC activity will take place in a group setting. As with nearly everything, the group process can be made more effective by acquiring a better understanding of the way it works.

The group process

Human beings are social by nature. People tend to seek out the company of other people. This is a great strength of our species, one that enabled us to rise above and dominate beasts much larger and stronger than ourselves. It is this ability that allowed men to control herds of livestock, to hunt swift antelope, and to protect themselves against predators. However, as natural as it is to belong to a group, there are certain behaviors that can make the group function more (or less) effectively.

We will define a group as a collection of individuals who share one or more common characteristics. The characteristic shared may be simple geography, i.e. the individuals are gathered together in the same place at the same time. Perhaps the group shares a common ancestry, like a family. Modern society consists of many different types of groups. The first group we join is, of course, our family. We also belong to groups of friends, sporting teams, churches, PTA's, and so on. The groups differ in many ways. They have different purposes, different time frames, and involve varying numbers of people. However, all effective groups share certain common features. In their work, "Joining Together", Johnson and Johnson list the following characteristics of an effective group:

- Group goals must be clearly understood, be relevant to the needs of group members, and evoke from every member a high level of commitment to their accomplishment.

- Group members must communicate their ideas and feelings accurately and clearly. Effective, two-way communication is the basis of all group functioning and interaction among group members.

- Participation and leadership must be distributed among members. All should participate, and all should be listened to. As leadership needs arise, members should all feel responsibility for meeting them. The equalization of participation and leadership makes certain that all members will be involved in the group's work, committed to implementing the group's decisions, and satisfied with their membership. It also assures that the resources of every member will be fully utilized, and increases the cohesiveness of the group.

- Appropriate decision-making procedures must be used flexibly if they are to be matched with the needs of the situation. There must be a balance between the availability of time and resources (such as member's skills) and the method of decision making used for making the decision. The most effective way of making a decision is usually by consensus (unanimous agreement). Consensus promotes distributed participation, the equalization of power, productive controversy, cohesion, involvement, and commitment.

- Power and influence need to be approximately equal throughout the group. They should be based on expertise, ability, and access to information, not on authority. Coalitions that help fulfill personal goals

13

should be formed among group members on the basis of mutual influence and interdependence.

- Conflicts arising from opposing ideas and opinions (controversy) are to be **encouraged**. Controversies promote involvement in the group's work, quality, creativity in decision making, and commitment to implementing the group's decisions. Minority opinions should be accepted and used. Conflicts prompted by incompatible needs or goals, by the scarcity of a resource (money, power), and by competitiveness must be negotiated in a manner that is mutually satisfying and does not weaken the cooperative interdependence of group members.

- Group cohesion needs to be high. Cohesion is based on members liking each other, each member's desire to continue as part of the group, the satisfaction of members with their group membership, and the level of acceptance, support, and trust among the members. Group norms supporting psychological safety, individuality, creativeness, conflicts of ideas, growth, and change need to be encouraged.

- Problem-solving adequacy should be high. Problems must be resolved with minimal energy and in a way that eliminates them permanently. Procedures should exist for sensing the existence of problems, inventing and implementing solutions, and evaluating the effectiveness of the solutions. When problems are dealt with adequately, the problem-solving ability of the group is increased, innovation is encouraged, and group effectiveness is improved.

- The interpersonal effectiveness of members needs to be high. Interpersonal effectiveness is a measure of how well the consequences of your behavior match intentions.

These attributes of effective groups apply regardless of the activity in which the group is engaged. It really doesn't matter if the group is involved in a study of air defense, or planning a prom dance. The common element is that there is a group of human beings engaged in pursuit of group goals.

Consensus decision rule

The first step in establishing an effective group is to create a consensus decision rule for the group, namely:

> **NO JUDGEMENT MAY BE INCORPORATED INTO THE GROUP DECISION UNTIL IT MEETS AT LEAST TACIT APPROVAL OF EVERY MEMBER OF THE GROUP.**

This minimum condition for group movement can be facilitated by adopting the following behaviors:

- Avoid arguing for your own position. Present it as lucidly and logically as possible, but be sensitive to and consider seriously the reactions of the group in any subsequent presentations of the same point.

- Avoid "win-lose" stalemates in the discussion of opinions. Discard the notion that someone must win and someone must lose in the discussion; when impasses occur, look for the next most acceptable alternative for all the parties involved.

- Avoid changing your mind only to avoid conflict and to reach agreement and harmony. Withstand pressures to yield which have no objective or logically sound foundation. Strive for enlightened flexibility; but avoid outright capitulation.

- Avoid conflict-reducing techniques such as the majority vote, averaging, bargaining, coin-flipping, trading out, and the like. Treat differences of opinion as indicative of an incomplete sharing of relevant information on someone's part, either about task issues, emotional data, or "gut level" intuitions.

- View differences of opinion as both natural and helpful rather than as a hindrance in decision making. Generally, the more ideas expressed, the greater the likelihood of conflict will be; but the richer the array of resources will be as well.

- View initial agreement as suspect. Explore the reasons underlying apparent agreements; make sure people have arrived at the same conclusions for either the same basic reasons or for complementary reasons before incorporating such opinions into the group decision.

- Avoid subtle forms of influence and decision modification; e.g., when a dissenting member finally agrees, don't feel that he must be "rewarded" by having his own way on some subsequent point.

- Be willing to entertain the possibility that your group can achieve all the foregoing and actually excel at its task; avoid doomsaying and negative predictions for group potential.

Collectively, the above steps are sometimes known as the "consensus technique." In tests it was found that 75% of the groups who were instructed in this approach significantly outperformed their best individual resources.

Stages in group development

Groups of many different types tend to evolve in similar ways. It often helps to know that the process of building an effective group is proceeding "normally." Bruce W. Tuckman identified four stages in the development of a group: forming, storming, norming, and performing.

During the *forming* stage a group tends to emphasize procedural matters. Group interaction is very tentative and polite. The leader dominates the decision making process and plays a very important role in moving the group forward.

The *storming* stage follows forming. Conflict between members, and between members and the leader, are characteristic of this stage. Members question authority as it relates to the group objectives, structure, or procedures. It is common for the group to resist the attempts of its leader to move them toward independence. Members are trying to define their role in the group. It is important that the leader deal with the conflict constructively. There are several ways in which this may be done:

- Do not tighten control or try to force members to conform to the procedures or rules established during the forming stage. If disputes over procedures arise, guide the group toward new procedures based on a group consensus.

- Probe for the true reasons behind the conflict and negotiate a more acceptable solution.

- Serve as a mediator between group members.

- Directly confront counterproductive behavior.

- Continue moving the group toward independence from its leader.

During the *norming* stage the group begins taking responsibility, or ownership, of its goals, procedures, and behavior. The focus is on working together efficiently. Group norms are enforced on the group by the group itself.

The final stage is *performing*. Members have developed a sense of pride in the group, its accomplishments, and their role in the group. Members are confident in their ability to contribute to the group and feel free to ask for or give assistance.

Productive group roles

There are two basic types of roles assumed by members of a group. *Group task roles* are one type. Group task roles are those functions concerned with facilitating and coordinating the group's efforts to select, define, and solve a particular problem. The following group task roles are generally recognized:

Initiator	Proposes new ideas, tasks or goals; suggests procedures or ideas for solving a problem or for organizing the group.
Information seeker	Asks for relevant facts related to the problem being discussed.
Opinion seeker	Seeks clarification of values related to problem or suggestion.
Information giver	Provides useful information about subject under discussion.
Opinion giver	Offers his/her opinion of suggestions made. Emphasis is on values rather than facts.
Elaborator	Gives examples.
Coordinator	Shows relationship among suggestions; points out issues and alternatives.
Orientor	Relates direction of group to agreed upon goals.
Evaluator	Questions logic behind ideas, usefulness of ideas, or suggestions.
Energizer	Attempts to keep the group moving toward an action.
Procedure technician	Keeps group from becoming distracted by performing such tasks as distributing materials, checking seating, etc..
Recorder	Serves as the "group memory."

The other type of role is the *group maintenance role*. Group maintenance roles are aimed at building group cohesiveness and group-centered behavior. They include:

Encourager	Offers praise of other members; accepts the contributions of others.
Harmonizer	Reduces tension by providing humor or by promoting reconciliation; gets people to explore their differences in a manner that benefits the entire group.

Compromiser	This role may be assumed when a group member's idea is challenged; admits errors, offers to modify his/her position.
Gate-keeper	Encourages participation, suggests procedures for keeping communication channels open.
Standard setter	Expresses standards for group to achieve, evaluates group progress in terms of these standards.
Observer/commentator	Records aspects of group process; helps group evaluate its functioning.
Follower	Passively accepts ideas of others; serves as audience in group discussions.

The development of task and maintenance roles is a vital part of the "team building process." Team building is defined as the process by which a group learns to function as a unit, rather than as a collection of individuals.

Counter-productive group roles

In addition to developing productive group oriented behavior it is also important to recognize and deal with individual roles which may block the building of a cohesive and effective team. These individual roles include the following:

Aggressor	Expresses disapproval by attacking the values, ideas, or feelings of other. Shows jealousy or envy.
Blocker	Prevents progress by persisting on issues that have been resolved; resists attempts at consensus; opposes without reason.
Recognition seeker	Calls attention to himself/herself by boasting, relating personal achievements, etc..
Confessor	Uses group setting as a forum to air personal ideologies that have little to do with group values or goals.
Playboy	Displays lack of commitment to group's work by cynicism, horseplay, etc..
Dominator	Asserts authority by interrupting others, using flattery to manipulate, claiming superior status.
Help-seeker	Attempts to evoke sympathy and/or assistance from other members through "poor me" attitude.

Special interest pleader   Asserts the interests of a particular group. This group's interest matches his/her self-interest.

The leader's role includes that of "process observer." In this capacity the leader monitors the atmosphere during group meetings and the behavior of individuals. The purpose is to identify counterproductive behavior. Of course, once identified, the leader must tactfully and diplomatically provide feedback to the group and its members. The success of SPC is, to a great extent, dependent on the performance of groups.

Management's role

Perhaps the most important thing management can do for a group is to give it time to become effective. This requires, among other things, that management work to maintain consistent group membership. Group members must not be moved out of the group without very good reason. Nor should there be a constant stream of new people "temporarily" assigned to the group. If a group is to progress through the four stages described earlier in this chapter, to the crucial *performing* stage, it will require a great deal of discipline from both the group and management.

Another area where management must help is creating an atmosphere within the company where groups can be effective. The methods for accomplishing this are beyond the scope of this book. However, one place to begin is Deming's 14 Points which are listed in chapter 1.

CHAPTER 3

DATA COLLECTION

Objectives

After completing this section you will:

- Understand the importance of data collection.
- Be able to locate sources of existing data.
- Know how to evaluate the validity of data.
- Be able to construct data collection sheets.
- Understand the different types of data.

Why collect data

Data can be collected for a variety of reasons. Some of the more common reasons are:

Descriptive data | This data is collected to obtain a more detailed description of some phenomenon. Often the problem is so poorly understood at the start that team members can't agree on whether a problem even exists. Descriptive data can be used to answer such basic questions.

Inferential data | Data is sometimes used to investigate cause and effect relationships. Don't think about this type of data too narrowly, we are not referring to science-class type experiments. Let's say, for example, that you think time on the job affects performance. If you obtain personnel records for a group of employees and use this to determine time on the job, then obtain manufacturing records to determine productivity, you've conducted an experiment (albeit a poorly controlled experiment). The conclusions reached as a result of analyzing this data are called "inferences."

SPC data

SPC relies on data to determine if a process has been influenced by a special cause. As you will learn in this book, without statistical tools this is more difficult than you might think. Processes produce variable output even when the process hasn't changed. SPC data helps you separate "signal" from "noise" and thus guides you to take appropriate action, which is often to take no action at all!

Acceptance data

When data is collected and compared to pre-established requirements (such as engineering specifications), and when product, materials, and processes are accepted or rejected based on this data, we call this acceptance data.

Sources of data

An early assignment for any SPC team is the definition of their project. Usually, management won't assign the team a specific project, instead they will give the team a charter that covers an area. The team must select their project from the area covered by their charter, and this will require data. Thus, the first task that faces the team is the acquisition of data. Among the many sources of data within any given company are:

Computer reports

Modern companies have such a large number of formal reports that it sometimes seems as if they are buried by them. It would be a shame to ignore this resource, especially since so much time, money, and effort is spent on it!

Manual reports

Many data sources are still written out by hand. Most departments have reports that are prepared periodically by hand to track important data that are difficult to put on a computer. Often, these reports are kept on file for past months and provide a valuable history.

Log books

Quite often data are never formally summarized in any report. Log books are one good example. When people seek to keep other people informed about topics of current interest, they often record the information in a log book. An example is the log books that supervisors use to tell the next shift about problems. These log books are very often goldmines to SPC teams trying to zero in on the best opportunity for improvement.

Special studies

SPC teams often find themselves in need of very detailed data regarding specific problems that have persisted for long periods of time. It is rare that some expert, or group of experts, within the company hasn't looked into just that problem. The team can save itself a great deal of work and embarrassment by checking into this before embarking on a special study of their own.

Vendor data

Vendors are usually more knowledgeable about their products and processes than the end user. Vendors also tend to keep records and often submit documentation with their shipments. Such information may reside in a variety of places, including laboratories, quality control files, purchasing files, or receiving files. At times the vendor must be asked to send additional data. Vendors are a source of expertise often overlooked.

Memos and notes

Much correspondence passes between employees in a company. The correspondence represents a tremendous source of factual information. Team members may remember key persons who corresponded with each other, with outside experts, or with vendors on a problem; these people should be asked to look through their files for data that will help the SPC team.

People's memory

Although written records are usually more reliable than memory, the possibility that a key person will remember important information should not be overlooked. Of course, when this information is recalled, it should be written down!

Obtaining new data

The team will probably find itself with two problems that appear to be conflicting: too much data, and not enough data. Typically, the company will have an abundance of management data, which the team will find very useful in developing a broad definition of their project. There will also be a tremendous amount of data available from such sources as engineers, data processing departments, vendors, laboratories, and other experts; data that cover specific elements in great detail. Both types of data are important and useful to their primary recipients. However, the data may or may not be useful to the team. The team must cull the wheat from the chaff, so to speak.

On the other side of the coin, the team will find that there is a great deal of essential data that does not exist. Chances are that the efforts of the company have been applied unevenly, and there are areas that have received less attention from management or in-house experts. SPC teams are usually established in these areas; in other words, the SPC program is a way to devote management attention and company expertise to an area that shows a need. The expertise is represented by the SPC team and others involved in the SPC project.

Variables, attributes, and rank-order data

Most of the data we will be using in the SPC program will fall into three different categories: variables, attributes, or rank-order. These groups are defined as follows:

Variables data	Data that are obtained from a continuous scale of measurement. Examples of variables data are weights, lengths, time, pH, temperature, etc.. Conceptually, variables data can be thought of as data that can take on any value on a given scale.
Attribute data	Attribute data result from counting. Some attribute data come from classifying objects into a limited number of categories. For example, product may be classified as grade A, grade B, or reject. Other attribute data may be just the counts themselves; examples of this would be typographical errors per sales order, or defects per square yard of carpet.
Rank-order data	At times it is very difficult to measure something, but it is relatively easy to determine a rank-order sequence. Examples of this are such things as flavors, appearance, pleasantness, etc.. A brand new Mercedes looks "better" than a beat up

Studebaker. The usefulness of such data should not be underestimated.

There are many things to consider when deciding which type of data to collect. Often, you can choose a measure of performance from any of several scales. Such things as cost, ease of data collection, need for skilled personnel, amount of detail required, and timeliness all need to be considered. Most important is to keep in mind the purpose of the data; the amount and type of data should be consistent with the use you plan to make of the data. An example of the different alternatives may help clarify things. Let's say that your team has evaluated cost data and determined that scrap on a precision machined shaft is a major concern. Also, a more detailed investigation has revealed that the biggest problem is that shafts that are too small are being produced. There are two options under consideration:

OPTION 1 Check the shaft diameter with a micrometer.

OPTION 2 Check the shaft by using a "go/not-go" gage. This is a gage designed so that shafts of the correct size will pass through the go part of the gage but will not pass through the not-go part of the gage.

There are many things to think about here, but the most important thing is to think about the purpose of the data. If you are doing a special study that involves a small number of parts or a short period of time, you will probably want to use Option 1, because a precise measurement of the diameter will give you more information than Option 2. If you plan to set up a permanent data system on a high-volume operation where the operator has limited time or skill levels, you will probably choose option 2. There are different techniques used to analyze the different types of data, but the choice of which type of data to collect should be made first - not the technique.

Data collection tools

The collection of data can be simplified by using the correct data collection tools. In fact, the tool itself can make the inspection process more reliable. Some time ago I attended a seminar where one of the speakers was the project quality manager for the first space shuttle. At the time, the shuttle had just entered the production stage and the quality people were busy trying to set up systems for quality control. One of their problems involved writing inspection instructions for complex electronic assemblies and several alternative methods were being tested. The test involved having a set of panels inspected by a group of experts composed of engineers, supervisors, and technicians. The group recorded their findings and the same panels were then checked by assemblers, solderers, testers, and inspectors. The results were then compared.

As you might expect for a project like the space shuttle, the biggest concern was "escapes." An escape is a defect that is missed by inspection. The study showed that escapes were quite high, even among the experts, and a group was commissioned to solve this problem. Among the things the group looked into was double and triple inspection, a costly alternative at best. Luckily, the group found a better way: the checklist. It was shown that if every possible defect was determined and documented on a well organized set of checklists, that escapes were dramatically reduced, to nearly zero. Of course, *preventing* defects is the only way to guarantee quality.

Checklists, work sheets, and other data collection aids can make the job of getting valid data much easier. Properly designed, these aids can even make the evaluation of the data a snap! Ideally, these sheets will reduce the amount of writing and calculating to a minimum, while still providing a maximum amount of information. There are several basic principles and methods to keep in mind when designing a data collection sheet.

Layout of data sheets

The sheet should be laid out so the data recording process proceeds in a logical way. Normally, a sheet that involves completing items in a top-to-bottom, left-to-right manner has the most appeal. If calculations are required, the sheet should make it easy to see what the calculations are and in what order they should be performed. Be sure you leave enough room to write in the required data; few things are more frustrating than trying to put too much data in too little space. Figure 3.1 shows the layout of a typical data collection sheet.

Header   A good data collection sheet should have a header that clearly identifies the sheet and where it is to be used. The header displays the name of the sheet, the process being monitored, the time period covered, and other data that will remain constant for the entire sheet.

Instructions   The form's instructions should be clearly written and readily available for the user of the form. If

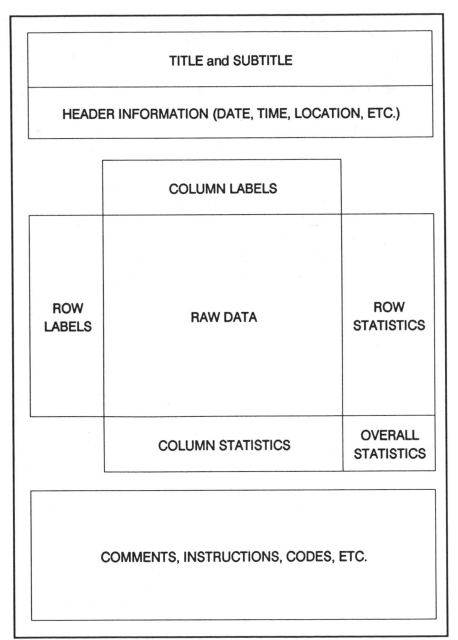

Figure 3.1 - Layout of a Typical Data Sheet

possible, the instructions should be written on the form itself, perhaps on the rear of the page.

Codes
Most of the time you will find that there are some things that happen over and over again. When this occurs you can probably save time by creating a code for identifying the repeating condition. The codes may identify the operator, a shift, a defect type, a defect location, a vendor, etc..

Location diagrams

Pictures, as you may have heard, are worth a thousand words. By using flow charts, part drawings, and other devices, you will often be able to determine patterns in the data that would be impossible to see otherwise. These patterns can be helpful in solving problems. It is often useful to take a photograph of the part and then mark the location of the defects on the picture. The same approach can be used with plant layout blueprints for analyzing the location in the plant where accidents, handling damage, defects of a certain type, etc. occurs. In one case an SPC team used a department layout diagram and marked the number of occurrences of dust contamination of a particular hybrid microcircuit. The team noticed that the defect pattern seemed highest near the entrance to the department. An investigation showed that the door to the clean room's airlock had been propped open with a paint can! It seems that the inconvenience of going in and out of the airlock was too much for some of the employees.

Check-off sheets

When all possible conditions can be described and listed, the data collection process can often be reduced to placing a check mark in the appropriate place on the form. This serves two purposes: it makes sure the item will be considered, and it makes the data recording process easier.

CHAPTER 4

PROBLEM SOLVING TECHNIQUES

Objectives

After completing this section you will be able to:

- Participate in brainstorming sessions.
- Create and understand process flow charts.
- Construct and interpret cause and effect diagrams.

Introduction

First of all, we need to define terms. **Problem solving** is defined as the process of discovering the cause of some undesirable event and taking action to eliminate the cause. The undesirable event might be defective parts, variation in the thickness of a washer, or invoices paid late.

As you can see from the definition, we are going to concentrate on the root cause. Far too often groups go astray by treating the effects rather than the causes. Here's an example. An SPC project had been conducted on a wave solder process. After about a year the team had managed to reduce the solder defect rate to less than a tenth of its former level while increasing productivity five-fold. I was attending a presentation of these results to the executive staff of a large defense contractor. After the presentation one of the executives challenged the team leader to justify his choice of the wave solder area for the project, stating, "For crying out loud, solder defects aren't even a problem. We haven't had a single line stop due to solder defects!" In fact, that was true. However, as the leader pointed out, there were reasons why the solder area was selected. Chiefly, 40% of the resources spent on soldering went to inspection and repair. That figure included floor area, equipment, and labor. The problem existed, but all of the "pain signals" had been destroyed by allocating resources to deal with the effects. Consider the money spent to manage the problem as a pain-killing drug. No self-respecting doctor would consider the patient cured simply because he had adminstered a pain-killer. But this practice is quite common in business, and it is the reason you must approach the problem solving process methodically. If you rely on your intuition alone to guide you in the problem solving effort there is a very good chance that you'll be attracted by pain signals. You may be solving the biggest *current problem* while much more costly problem areas are ignored.

Critical and creative thinking

This book will emphasize both creative and critical thinking processes. You would be mistaken to believe that one type of thinking is "better" or "worse" than the other - in any given situation you may need one or the other, or both. Critical thinking is the type of thinking stressed in virtually all of our formal education. It is the type of thinking we are using when we look for a "correct answer" using the "correct method." It emphasises a step-by-step, logical approach. When using critical thinking we are, in effect, considering a variety of possible solutions and trying to home in on the best solution. According to scientists this type of thinking takes place mainly in the left side of the brain. Creative thinking is much different than critical thinking and most people have had little or no training in creative thinking. It is less structure and attempts to identify possibilities rather than correct answers. Where critical thinking seeks the correct, creative thinking makes use of the wild guess. Where critical thinking emphasises convergence on the best answer, creative thinking looks for divergence to answers that may appear to be far out and impractical. Creative thinking brings the right side of the brain into the problem solving process. What the right side lacks in logic it more than makes up for in imagination!
The two types of thinking require totally different approaches and both are necessary. The reason critical thinking alone may fail is obvious when you consider that it is a convergent approach. This implies that you are implicitly evaluating a set of alternatives with the objective of choosing the best alternative. If you do this before you employ creative thinking the chances are good that the set of alternatives may not contain the best alternative. The diver-

gent nature of creative thinking makes it more likely that the best alternative will be considered.

Brainstorming

Brainstorming is a process designed to draw out the collective knowledge of a group. The problem solving techniques described in this chapter will all be more productive if the rules of brainstorming are followed first.

There are four basic rules that govern brainstorming sessions:

No criticism	The discussion leader must enforce this rule very strictly. Creative new ideas are never complete and it is far too easy to criticize them and kill them. Critical evaluation of ideas must wait for a later session.
Get wild	Brainstorming is a time to let your mind soar! Don't settle for safe, practical ideas. Great improvements require great leaps ahead. Imagine how wild such things as satellite TV and microwave ovens would have sounded 50 years ago.
Quantity, not quality	All we want is a large number of ideas here, we don't care if they're good or bad. The greater the idea count, the better.
Combinations are o.k.	If you see that two or more previous suggestions could be combined somehow, say so. This is a team effort and no one should feel that "he stole my idea."

The leader should make it a point to solicit everyone's contribution. This is done by going from person to person in rotation. If a member doesn't have an idea on a particular round, he simply says "I pass." However, he is asked on every round.

A final point, the human mind thinks at two different levels, the conscious and the unconscious. After a good brainstorming session everyone's mind will be spinning with all of the new, wild ideas. The unconscious mind will continue brainstorming even after you've stopped thinking about it at a conscious level. Thus, the team should continue the brainstorming after an "incubation period" has passed.

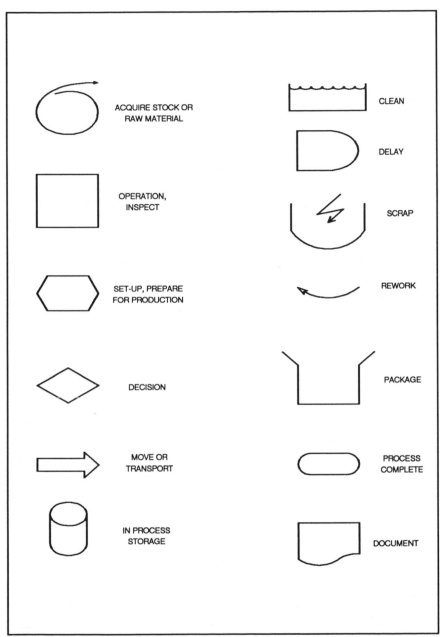

Figure 4.1 Flow Chart Symbols

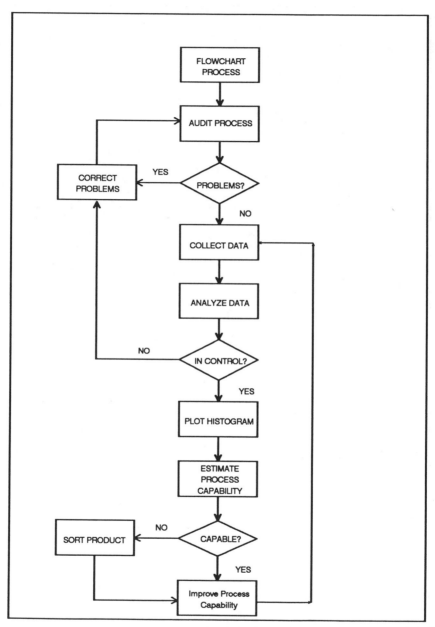

Figure 4.2 Flow Chart of a Typical SPC Project

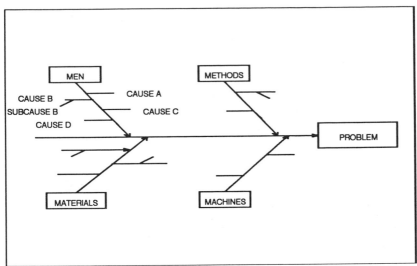

Figure 4.3 - Generic Cause & Effect Diagram

Flowcharting

When you begin your project you will immediately find that each member of the team possesses different knowledge relating to your goals. One of your tasks will be to collect and organize everyone's knowledge so the entire group has the same level of understanding. One of the most useful methods for organizing a group's knowledge of a process is the process flowchart. A process flowchart is simply a tool that graphically shows the inputs, actions, and outputs of a given system. These terms are defined as follows:

Inputs	The factors of production. Conventionally, inputs can be classified into 4 broad categories: land, labor, equipment, and management.
Actions	The way in which the inputs are combined. Actions include procedures, handling, storage, transportation, and processing.
Outputs	The product or service created by the actions taken on the inputs.

Flowcharting is such a useful activity that the symbols used for flowcharts have been standardized. The common flowchart symbols are shown in figure 4.1. Some of the flowchart symbols apply to information processing, while others are used for manufacturing. However, since nearly all quality improvement projects need to consider both information processes and physical processes, both types of symbols are shown.

Figure 4.2 shows a simplified example of a flowchart for the SPC process. The flowchart can be made either more complex or less complex. Generally the tendency is for the flowchart to start out rather simple and to become more complex as more is learned about the process. As a rule of thumb, make the flowchart only as complex as is necessary to help you understand the basic process. It is not necessary to include every little detail on the flowchart. In fact, excessively complex flowcharts tend to create confusion, exactly the opposite of what we want. We will discuss other techniques for organizing detailed process information later in this book.

Cause and effect diagrams

Cause and effect diagrams, originally developed by Dr. Kaoru Ishikawa, [1] are tools that are used to organize and graphically display all of the knowledge a group has relating to a particular problem. Usually, the steps are:

1. Develop a flow chart of the process to be improved.

2. Carefully define the problem to be solved.

3. Brainstorm to find all possible causes of the problem.

4. Organize the brainstorming results into rational categories.

5. Construct a cause and effect diagram that accurately displays the relationships of all the data in each category.

The cause and effect diagram is very simple to construct. After completing the 5 steps above, the steps necessary to construct the cause and effect diagram are:

1. Draw a box on the far right hand side of a large sheet of paper and draw a horizontal arrow that points to the box. Inside of the box, write the description of the problem you are trying to solve.

2. Write the names of the categories above and below the horizontal line. Think of these as branches from the main trunk of the tree.

---

1   Ishikawa, K.,"Guide to Quality Control, Second Revised Edition," Unipub / Quality Resources, White Plains, NY, 1986

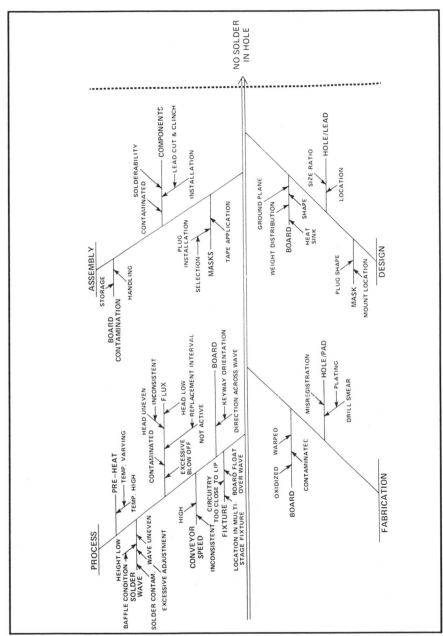

Figure 4.4 - Sample Cause & Effect Diagram

3. Draw in the detailed cause data for each category. Think of these as limbs and twigs on the branches. figure 4.3 depicts a "generic cause and effect diagram."

A good cause and effect diagram will have many "twigs." If your cause and effect diagram doesn't have a lot of smaller branches and twigs, it shows that the understanding of the problem is superficial. Chances are you need the help of someone outside of your group to aid in the understanding, perhaps someone more closely associated with the problem. Figure 4.4 shows a cause and effect diagram created by an SPC team working on a soldering problem. Cause and effect diagrams have a number of uses. Creating the diagram is an education in itself. Organizing the knowledge of the group serves as a guide for discussion and frequently inspires more ideas. The cause and effect diagram, once created, acts as a record of your research. Simply record your tests and results as you proceed. If the true cause is found to be something that wasn't on the original diagram, write it in. Finally, the cause and effect diagram is a display of your current level of understanding. It shows the existing level of technology as understood by the team. It is a good idea to post the cause and effect diagram in a prominent location for all to see.

As mentioned earlier, cause and effect diagrams, like most SPC techniques, are tools designed to aid *critical thinking*. The inputs that are organized on these diagrams can obtained best by using the *creative thinking* technique of brainstorming before starting construction of the cause and effect diagram. Brainstorming will make it more likely that all possible causes are considered.

CEDAC

A variation of the basic cause and effect diagram, developed by Dr. Ryuji Fukuda,[2] is cause and effect diagrams with the addition of cards, or CEDAC. The main difference is that the group can also gather ideas outside of the meeting room. The ideas are written on small cards. The cards also serve as a vehicle for gathering input from people who are not in the group, they can be distributed to anyone involved with the process. Often the cards provide more information than the brief entries on a standard cause and effect

---

2   Fukuda, Ryuji, Managerial Engineering, Productivity, Inc., Stamford, Connecticut, 1983

diagram. The cause and effect diagram is built by actually placing the cards on the branches.

CHAPTER 5

FUNDAMENTAL SPC CONCEPTS

Objectives

After completing this section you will:

- Know the difference between variation from special causes and variation from common causes.

- Understand distributions.

- Know how to represent variation in a process.

- Understand the difference between problem prevention and problem management.

- Understand why meeting requirements is not good enough.

In his landmark book, *Economic Control of Quality of Manufactured Product*, Shewhart described the following: [1]

> *"Write the letter "a" on a piece of paper. Now make another a just like the first one; then another and another until you have a series of a's,a,a,a,... You try to make all the a's alike but you don't; you can't. You are willing to accept this as an empirically established fact. But what of it? Let us see just what this means in respect to control. Why can we not do a simple thing like making all the a's exactly alike? Your answer leads to a generalization which all of us are perhaps willing to accept. It is that there are many causes of variability among the a's: the paper was not smooth, the lead in the pencil was not uniform, and the unavoidable variability in your external surroundings reacted*

---

1   Shewhart, W.A., Economic Control of Quality of Manufactured Product, ASQC. Milwaukee, Wisconsin, originally published in 1931, reprinted in 1980.

upon you to introduce variation in the a's. But are these the only causes of variability in the a's? Probably not.

"We accept our human limitations and say that likely there are many other factors. If we could but name all the reasons why we cannot make the a's alike, we would most assuredly have a better understanding of a certain part of nature than we now have. Of course, this conception of what it means to be able to do what we want to do is not new; it does not belong exclusively to any one field of human thought; it is commonly accepted.

*"The point to be made in this simple illustration is that we are limited in doing what we want to do; that to do what we set out to do, even in so simple a thing as making a's that are alike, requires almost infinite knowledge compared with that which we now possess. It follows, therefore, since we are thus willing to accept as axiomatic that we cannot do what we want to do and cannot hope to understand why we cannot, that we must also accept as axiomatic that a controlled quality will not be a constant quality. Instead, a controlled quality must be a **variable** quality. This is the first characteristic.*

"But let us go back to the results of the experiment on the a's and we shall find out something more about control. Your a's are different from my a's; there is something about your a's that makes them yours and something about my a's that makes them mine. True, not all of your a's are alike. Neither are all of my a's alike. Each group of a's varies within a certain range and yet each group is distinguishable from the others. This distinguishable and, as it were, constant variability **within limits** *is the second characteristic of control."*

Shewhart goes on to define control:

"A phenomenon will be said to be controlled when, through the use of past experience, we can predict, at least within limits, how the phenomenon may be expected to vary in the future. Here it is understood that prediction within limits means that we can state, at least approximately, the probability that the observed phenomenon will fall within the given limits."

The critical point in this definition is that control is not defined as the complete absence of variation. Control is simply a state where all variation is predictable variation. In all forms of prediction there is an element of chance. Any unknown cause of variation is called a *chance cause.* If the influence of any particular chance cause is very small, and if the number of chance causes of variation are very large and relatively constant, we have a situation where the variation is predictable within limits. You can see from our definition above that a system such as this qualifies as a controlled system. Deming uses the term *common cause* rather than chance cause, and we will use common cause in this book.

An example of such a controlled system might be the production and distribution of peaches. If you went into an orchard to a particular peach tree at the right time of the year, you would find a tree laden with peaches (with any luck at all). The weights of the peaches will vary. However, if you weighed every single peach on the tree you would probably notice that there was a distinct pattern to the weights. In fact, if you drew a small random sample of, say, 25 peaches you could probably predict the weights of those peaches remaining on the tree. This predictability is the essence of a controlled phenomenon. The number of common causes that account for the variation in peach weights is astronomical, but relatively constant. A constant system of common causes results in a controlled phenomenon.

Needless to say, not all phenomena arise from constant systems of common causes. At times the variation is caused by a source of variation that is not part of the constant system. These sources of variation were called **assignable causes** by Shewhart, Deming calls them **special causes** of variation. Experience indicates that special causes of variation can usually be found and eliminated.

Statistical tools are needed to help us effectively identify the effects of special causes of variation. This leads us to another definition:

*Statistical process control (SPC)*is defined as the use of statistical methods to identify the existence of special causes of variation in a process.

The basic rule of Statistical Process Control is:

> *VARIATION FROM COMMON CAUSE SYSTEMS SHOULD BE LEFT TO CHANCE, BUT SPECIAL CAUSES OF VARIATION SHOULD BE IDENTIFIED AND ELIMINATED.*

The charts in figure 5.1 illustrate the need for statistical methods to determine the category of variation. The answer to the question "should these variations be left to chance?" can be obtained through the use of statistical theory. Figure 5.2 illustrates the basic concept. Variation between the "control limits" designated by the two lines will be considered to be variation from the common cause system. Any variability beyond these limits will be treated as having come from special causes of variation. We will call any sys-

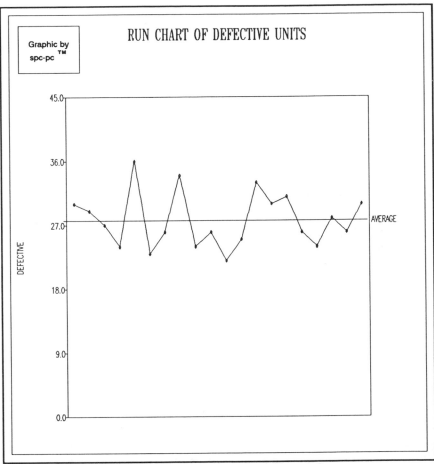

Figure 5.1-Should These Variations Be Left to Chance?

tem exhibiting only common cause variation "statistically controlled." It must be noted that the control limits are not simply pulled out of the air, they are calculated from statistical theory. A control chart is a practical tool that provides an operational definition of a special cause.

Distributions

A fundamental concept of statistical process control is that almost every measurable phenomenon is a statistical distribution. In other words, an ob-

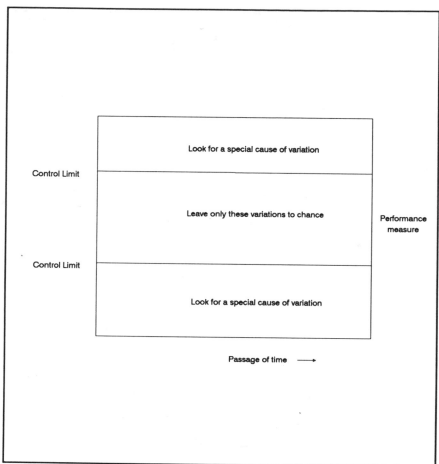

Figure 5.2-Basic Concept of Control Charts

served set of data constitutes a sample of the effects of unknown common causes. It follows that, after we have done everything to eliminate special causes of variations, there will still remain a certain amount of variability exhibiting the state of control. Figure 5.3 illustrates the relationships between common causes, special causes, and distributions.

There are three basic properties of a distribution: location, spread, and shape. The distribution can be characterized by these three parameters. Figure 5.4 illustrates these three properties. The location refers to the typical value of the distribution. The spread of the distribution is the amount by

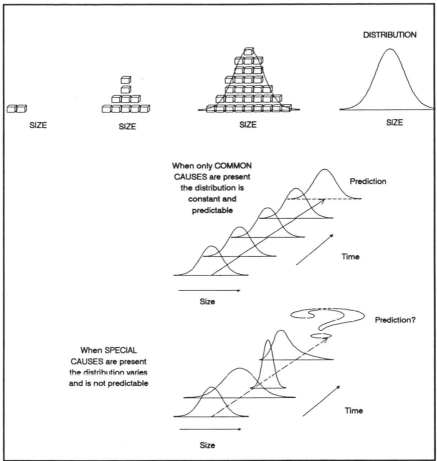

Figure 5.3-Common and Special Causes and Distributions

which smaller values differ from larger ones. And the shape of a distribution is its pattern - peakedness, symmetry, etc.. Note that a given phenomenon may have any of a number of distributions, i.e. the distribution may be bell-shaped, rectangular shaped, etc.. In this book we will discuss methods which facilitate the analysis and control of distributions.

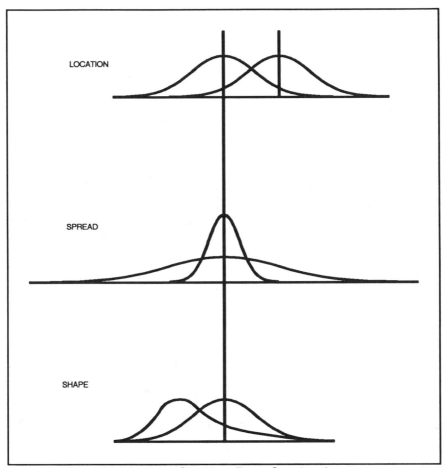

Figure 5.4-How Distributions Can Vary From One Another

Normal distribution

Even though there are a variety of distributions that we can expect to find, one particular distribution tends to appear over and over again. The distribution is so common, in fact, that it has been given the name "Normal Distribution." The normal distribution curve is shown in figure 5.5.

Central limit theorem

The normal distribution has been studied intensively. Its utility has been enhanced by the creation of tables. We will use the normal distribution exten-

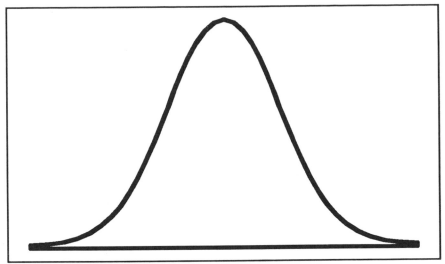

Figure 5.5-The Normal Distribution

sively in this book. The central limit theorem will greatly extend the usefulness of the normal distribution.

The central limit theorem can be stated as follows:

*Irrespective of the shape of the distribution of the universe, the distribu-
tion of average values of samples drawn from that universe will tend
toward a normal distribution as the sample size grows without bound.*

The "universe" is the group we are concerned with. In the SPC situation it is
typically the process we are measuring. A logical question is how large the
sample size must be for the central limit theorem to work. Shewhart performed experiments that showed that relatively small sample sizes, 4 to 6 observations per sample, would produce approximately normal distributions
from even wildly non-normal universes. Figure 5.6 illustrates the effect of the
central limit theorem on a non-normal distribution. Note that the spread of
the distribution of averages is less than that of the original distribution and
the shape of the distribution of averages is approximately normal.

The practical implications of the central limit theorem and Shewhart's
demonstration are immense. Without the central limit theorem's effects you
would have to develop a separate model for every non-normal distribution
you encounter. This would be the only way to determine if the system were

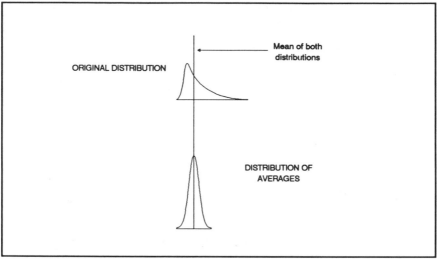

Figure 5.6-Illustration Central Limit Theorem Effect

exhibiting chance variation. Because of the central limit theorem you can use **averages** of small samples to evaluate **any** process using the normal distribution. The central limit theorem provides the basis of one of the most powerful of statistical process control tools, Shewhart control charts. Shewhart control charts are covered in chapters 8 – 10.

Measures of central tendency

As stated above, measurements from a process can be represented by a distribution. The distribution, in turn, can be characterized by its location, spread, and shape. The location of a distribution is its "typical value." The term typical value is not precise enough for SPC, it can mean different things to different people. We will use statistics to help us determine the typical value.

When we talk about the **location** of a distribution in this book we are referring to the central tendency of the distribution. Remember that a distribution is the pattern that remains after we have eliminated all special causes of variation. This definition implies that we have obtained a reasonably large number of samples, analyzed their pattern, and found that they exhibit variation that could arise from a common cause system. What might a typical value from this common cause system be?

There are several possible answers to the question. Intuitively, the value that divides the data into two equal parts is a typical value. This is known as the median. The median is calculated as follows:

Steps for Finding the Median

1. Sort the data from smallest to largest.
2. If the count of values is an odd number, then the median is the middle value. For example, if you have 5 numbers the median is the third value. The example below illustrates this.

DATA: 4.3, 3.2, 1.1, 4.0, 2.2.

RANK	VALUE
1	1.1
2	2.2
3	3.2 ← median = 3.2
4	4.0
5	4.3

3. If the count of values is an even number, then the median is obtained by dividing the sum of the two middle values by 2. For example

DATA: 4.3, 1.1, 4.0, 2.2

RANK	VALUE
1	1.1
2	2.2
3	4.0
4	4.3

$$\tilde{x} = \frac{2.2 + 4.0}{2} = 3.1 \tag{5.1}$$

Note that the symbol for the median is shown as $\tilde{x}$. In this book we will make frequent use of mathematical symbols as a shorthand way of referring to statistical quantities. Also notice the number (5.1) to the right of the equation. This is the number of the equation. All new equations will be given a

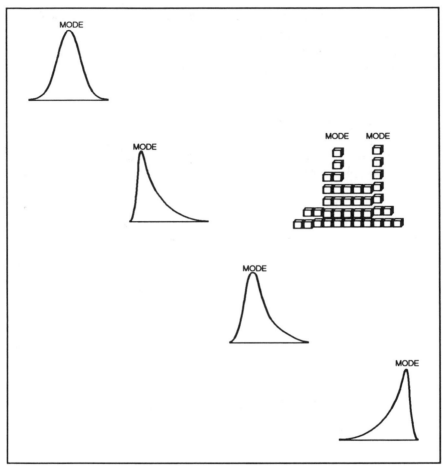

Figure 5.7-The Mode

number and the number may be used elsewhere in this book to refer to the
equation.

Another typical value might be the number that occurs most often. The
statistical term for this value is the mode. Figure 5.7 illustrates the mode.
Note that it is possible to have more than one mode. However, most of the
time a multiple mode situation indicates an out of control process. A process
with two modes is called "bimodal," one with three modes is called
"trimodal." The mode is useful in troubleshooting work, especially when
using histograms as a troubleshooting aid. This is discussed in chapter 6.

The final typical value we will consider here is the mean, or average value. It is found by adding up all of the values and dividing the sum by the count. Mathematically, here is how we state this:

$$\bar{x} = \frac{1}{n} \sum_{i=1}^{n} x_i \qquad (5.2)$$

For example, with the 4 data points used for the median example above, the mean would be

$$\bar{x} = \frac{4.3 + 1.1 + 4.0 + 2.2}{4} = \frac{11.6}{4} = 2.9$$

Observe that in this example the mean and the median are not the same. This may or may not be true with other data. Also, the data do not need to be sorted to compute the mean. Another thing to note is that the mean uses all of the numbers while the median only uses the middle one or two values. Thus, the mean is much more sensitive to "freak values" than the median. Nevertheless, the mean is the most commonly used typical value, or measure of central tendency of a distribution. The mean is the center of gravity of a distribution. We will occasionally make use of the median in this book, but the mean will be used far more often.

Measures of dispersion

The second property of a distribution that we want to measure is its spread, or dispersion. There are a number of useful statistics that quantify a distribution's spread. The easiest measure of dispersion to calculate is the range.

$$R = Largest - Smallest \qquad (5.3)$$

Fortunately, in addition to being easy to compute, the range is also one of the most useful statistics. Another measure of dispersion is the standard deviation, also known as sigma.

$$s = \sqrt{\sum_{i=1}^{n} \frac{(x_i - \overline{x})^2}{n-1}} \qquad (5.4)$$

Equation 5.4 is obviously more complicated than equation 5.3. Fortunately, when the distribution is from a constant system of chance causes, that is when the process is in statistical control, we can use the average range to obtain a very satisfactory estimate of s. The method for doing this is discussed in volume two of this series. Equation 5.4 will give inflated estimates of sigma when the process is out of control because it will include variation from the special causes.

Prevention versus detection

A process control system is essentially a feedback system. There are four main elements involved: the process itself, information about the process, action taken on the process, and action taken on the output from the process. The way these elements fit together is shown in figure 5.8.

By the process, we mean the whole combination of people, equipment, materials, methods, and environment that work together to produce output. The performance information is obtained, in part, from evaluation of the process output. The output of a process includes more than product, output also includes information about the operating state of the process such as temperature, cycle times, etc.. Action taken on a process is *future-oriented* in the sense that it will affect output yet to come. Action on the output is *past-oriented* because it involves detecting out-of-specification output that has already been produced.

Past-oriented strategies are problem *management* systems. Future-oriented strategies are problem *prevention* systems.

Historically, industry has concentrated its attention on the past-oriented, problem management strategy of inspection. With this approach we wait until output has been produced, then the output is inspected and either accepted or rejected. It should be very obvious that this does nothing to prevent substandard output in the future. This book takes you in a completely different direction: improvement of the process in the future, or problem prevention.

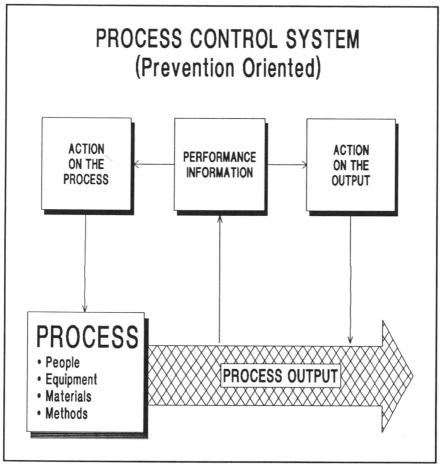

Figure 5.8-A Process Control System Feedback Loop

Process control versus meeting requirements

In the past-oriented world the emphasis was on meeting requirements. Such programs as zero defects received a great deal of attention because we were only concerned with producing output that met the minimum requirements. Anything that met requirements was acceptable, anything that failed requirements was unacceptable. This point of view is shown in figure 5.9
It is not hard to show that this view of loss is naive.

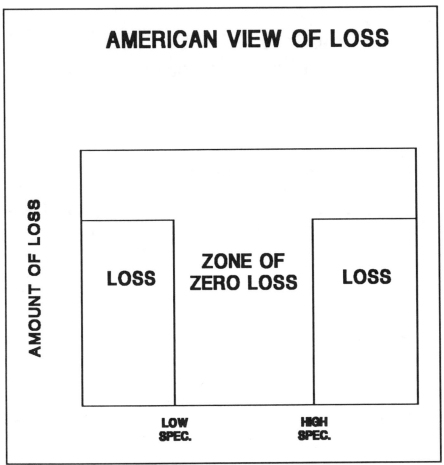

Figure 5.9-Model of Specification Based Control System

In most real world applications there is a "preferred" level of performance. When a process is performing at this preferred level, or target level, it runs smoother, costs less to maintain, and produces better quality output. This situation has been frequently demonstrated empirically. A more realistic

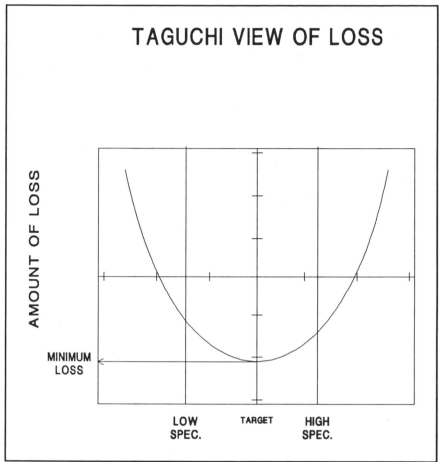

Figure 5.10-Model of Taguchi's Loss Function

model based on this school of thought was developed by Dr. Genichi Taguchi of Japan.[2] Figure 5.10 illustrates Taguchi's loss function.

This diagram shows that an optimum exists at some target value. The target may or may not be at the center of the specifications. Often the location of

2   Taguchi, G., System of Experimental Design, Kraus International, White Plains, New York, 1987

the target depends on the amount of variability in the process. For example, if very tight control of a bolt hole diameter can be maintained it may be wise to run the diameter to the small end of the specification to obtain a better fit. Furthermore, *the smaller the variation around the target, the smaller the total loss.* Thus, according to the Taguchi school of thought, it is not enough to merely meet the requirements. Continuous improvement is called for. Although Dr. Taguchi's methods go far beyond SPC, the concept of never ending, continuous improvement by reducing variation is also at the heart of the SPC approach. Meeting requirements is a side benefit. In fact, specifications are viewed simply as the point where it becomes more economical to scrap or rework than it is to ship. Specifications are only points on the loss function curve. With SPC and Taguchi methods quality levels will improve far beyond the marginal quality represented by specifications.

CHAPTER 6

DESCRIPTIVE DATA ANALYSIS

Objectives
After completing this section you will:

- Be able to perform Pareto analysis.
- Be able to construct and interpret histograms.
- Be able to construct and interpret scatter plots.

Pareto analysis

Definition   Pareto analysis is the process of ranking opportunities to determine which of many potential opportunities should be pursued first. It is also known as "separating the vital few from the trivial many."

Usage   Pareto analysis should be used at various stages in a quality improvement program to determine which step to take next. Pareto analysis is used to answer such questions as "What department should have the next SPC team?" or "On what type of defect should we concentrate our efforts?"

How to perform Pareto analysis
1. Determine the classifications (Pareto categories) for the graph. If the desired information does not exist, obtain it by designing checksheets and logsheets (see chapter 3).
2. Select a time interval for analysis. The interval should be long enough to be representative of typical performance.
3. Determine the total occurrences (i.e. cost, defect counts, etc.) for each category. Also determine the grand total. If there are several categories which account for only a small part of the total, group these into a category called "other."

4. Compute the percentage for each category by dividing the category total by the grand total and multiplying by 100.
5. Rank order the categories from the largest total occurrences to the smallest.
6. Compute the cumulative percentage by adding the percentage for each category to that of any preceding categories.
7. Construct a chart with the left vertical axis scaled from 0 to at least the grand total. Put an appropriate label on the axis. Scale the right vertical axis from 0 to 100%, with 100% on the right side being the same height as the grand total on the left side.
8. Label the horizontal axis with the category names. The leftmost category should be the largest, second largest next, and so on. If there is insufficient room to spell out the names, label the axis with the ranks of each category and include a key with the Pareto diagram.
9. Draw in bars representing the amount of each category. The height of the bar is determined by the left vertical axis.
10. Draw a line that shows the cumulative percentage column of the Pareto analysis table. The cumulative percentage line is plotted against the right vertical axis.

Example of Pareto analyses:

The data in table 6.1 has been recorded for peaches arriving at Super Duper Market during August. A Pareto analysis of these results will be performed according to the instructions above.

Table 6.1-Raw Data for Pareto Analysis

Problem	Peaches Lost
Bruised	100
Undersized	87
Rotten	235
Under-ripe	9
Wrong Variety	7
Wormy	3

Step 1.   Determine the classifications. The classifications will be the problems, e.g. bruised, under sized, etc..

Step 2.   Select a time interval. We will use the August data provided. Of course, if we didn't think August data were sufficient we could choose to go back to July.

Step 3.   Determine the total occurrences for each category. This has
            been done for us. In the real world we might need to go
            through, for example, daily records to get these totals. The
            grand total is found by adding all of the category totals, and it is
            441 peaches.

            Next we will group several categories accounting for small
            amounts into a category called "other." With our data we will
            place under-ripe, wrong variety, and wormy into "other" for a
            total of 19 peaches.

Step 4.   Compute the percentage for each category. The instructions so
            far result in table 6.2.

            As an example of the percentage calculation for rotten peaches,

            $\%rotten = 100 \times \dfrac{235}{441} = 53.29$. Note that, as often happens, the

            total of the percentage column is not exactly 100% due to round-
            off error. When this occurs it is nothing to worry about.

Step 5.   Sort the data from largest to smallest according to the count.

Step 6.   Compute the cumulative percentage. The sorted data and
            cumulative percentage column are shown in table 6.3.

Table 6.2-Raw Data and Percentage Column

Category	Count	Percentage
Bruised	100	22.68
Rotten	235	53.29
Under Sized	87	19.73
Other	19	4.31
TOTAL	**441**	**100.01**

Steps 7 - 10 Construct a bar/line chart of the data in table 6.3. Place counts
              on the left hand axis and cumulative percent on the right hand
              axis. Plot the bars against the left hand axis and the line against
              the right hand axis. This chart is shown in figure 6.1.

Related techniques

Pareto analysis is a simple but extremely powerful graphic technique. It can
be used in conjunction with cause and effect diagrams to help determine

Table 6.3-Completed Pareto Table

Rank	Category	Count	%	Cumulative %
1	Rotten	235	53.29	53.29
2	Bruised	100	22.68	75.97
3	Under sized	87	19.73	95.70
4	Other	19	4.31	100.01

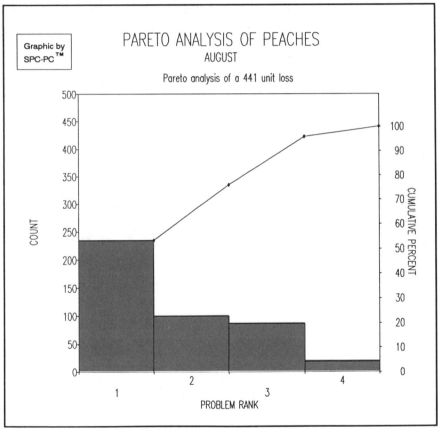

Figure 6.1-Completed **Pareto Diagram**

which of the many possible causes should be pursued first. Checksheets and logsheets frequently provide the source of data for Pareto analysis.

Pointers for Using Pareto analyses

- Pareto analysis can only be used when the category totals can be added together. In other cases, for example yields, Pareto analysis makes no sense.

- In many cases simple business charts such as line charts, bar charts, or pie charts should be used instead of or in addition to Pareto analysis.

- To be useful, Pareto analysis should give a chart where one or two categories dominate the chart. If the first several bars on your Pareto diagram are nearly the same height you should consider regrouping the data. Perhaps several categories can be grouped, for example could nicks, dents, and scratches all be grouped as "handling damage?" If regrouping fails to give a clear picture you may need to find a completely different classification scheme. For example, if classifying defects by the machine that they came from doesn't give a useful picture, try classifying defects by the material vendor, by shift, by part number, etc..

- Pareto analysis should be done on more than one performance measure. For example, if the cost of fixing an error varies according to the type of error, Pareto analysis should be done on both the number of errors and on the cost of errors.

Histograms

Definition   A histogram is a pictorial representation of a set of data. It is created by grouping the measurements into "cells."

Usage   Histograms are used to determine the shape of a data set. Also, a histogram displays the numbers in a way that makes it easy to see the dispersion and central tendency and to compare the distribution to requirements. Histograms can be valuable troubleshooting aids. Comparisons between histograms from different machines, operators, vendors, etc. often reveal important differences.

How to construct a histogram
1. Find the largest and the smallest value in the data.
2. Compute the range (see equation 5.3 in the previous chapter).

3. Select a number of cells for the histogram. Table 6.4 provides some useful guidelines. The final histogram may not have **exactly** the number of cells you choose here, as explained below.
4. Determine the width of each cell. We will use the letter W to stand for the cell width. W is computed from formula 6.1.

$$W = \frac{R}{\text{number of cells}} \qquad (6.1)$$

R was computed in step 2 above. The number W is a starting point. You should round W to a convenient number. Rounding W will affect the number of cells in your histogram.

5. Compute "cell boundaries." A cell is a range of values and cell boundaries define the start and end of each cell. Cell boundaries should have one more decimal place than the raw data values in the data set in

Table 6.4-Histogram Cell Determination Guidelines

Number of Values	Number of Cells in Histogram
100 or less	7 to 10
101 to 200	11 to 15
201 +	13 to 20

order to avoid ambiguities. The low boundary of the first cell must be less than the smallest value in the data set. Other cell boundaries are found by adding W to the previous boundary. Continue until the upper boundary is larger than the largest value in the data set.

6. Go through the raw data and determine into which cell each value falls. Mark a tick in the appropriate cell.
7. Count the ticks in each cell and record the count, also called the frequency, to the right of the tick marks.
8. Construct a graph from the table. The vertical axis of the graph will show the frequency in each cell. The horizontal axis will show the cell boundaries. Figure 6.2 illustrates the layout of a histogram.
9. Draw bars representing the cell frequencies. The bars should all be the same width, the height of the bars should equal the frequency in the cell.

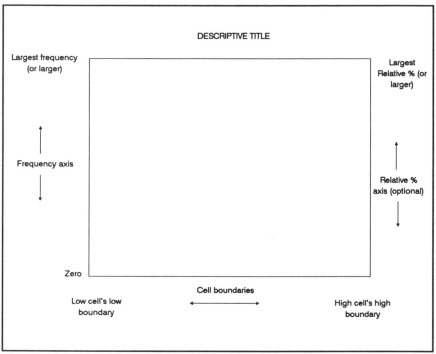

Figure 6.2-Layout of a Histogram

Histogram example

Assume you have the data in table 6.5 on the size of a metal rod. The rods were sampled every hour for 20 consecutive hours and 5 consecutive rods were checked each time (20 subgroups of 5 values per group).

Step 1   Find the largest and the smallest value in the data set. The smallest value is 0.982 and the largest is 1.021. Both values are marked with an (*) in table 6.5.

Step 2   Compute the range, R, by subtracting the smallest value from the largest value. $R = 1.021 - 0.982 = 0.039$.

Step 3   Select a number of cells for the histogram. Since we have 100 values 7 to 10 cells are recommended. We will use 10 cells.

Step 4   Determine the width of each cell, W. Using equation (6.1) we compute $W = 0.039 / 10 = 0.0039$. We will round this to 0.004 for convenience. Thus, $W = 0.004$.

Table 6.5-Data for Histogram

Row	Sample 1	Sample 2	Sample 3	Sample 4	Sample 5
1	1.002	0.995	1.000	1.002	1.005
2	1.000	0.997	1.007	0.992	0.995
3	0.997	1.013	1.001	0.985	1.002
4	0.990	1.008	1.005	0.994	1.012
5	0.992	1.012	1.005	0.985	1.006
6	1.000	1.002	1.006	1.007	0.993
7	0.984	0.994	0.998	1.006	1.002
8	0.987	0.994	1.002	0.997	1.008
9	0.992	0.988	1.015	0.987	1.006
10	0.994	0.990	0.991	1.002	0.988
11	1.007	1.008	0.990	1.001	0.999
12	0.995	0.989	0.982*	0.995	1.002
13	0.987	1.004	0.992	1.002	0.992
14	0.991	1.001	0.996	0.997	0.984
15	1.004	0.993	1.003	0.992	1.010
16	1.004	1.010	0.984	0.997	1.008
17	0.990	1.021*	0.995	0.987	0.989
18	1.003	0.992	0.992	0.990	1.014
19	1.000	0.985	1.019	1.002	0.986
20	0.996	0.984	1.005	1.016	1.012

Step 5   Compute the cell boundaries. The low boundary of the first cell must be below our smallest value of 0.982, and our cell boundaries should have one decimal place more than our raw data. Thus, the lower cell boundary for the first cell will be 0.9815. Other cell boundaries are found by adding $W = 0.004$ to the previous cell boundary until the upper boundary is greater than our largest value of 1.021. This gives us the cell boundaries in table 6.6.

Step 6   Go through the raw data and mark a tick in the appropriate cell for each data point.

Step 7   Count the tick marks in each cell and record the frequency to the right of each cell. The results of all we have done so far are shown in table 6.7. Table 6.7 is often referred to as a "frequency table" or "frequency tally sheet."

Steps 8-9   Construct a graph from the table in step 7. The frequency column will be plotted on the vertical axis, and the cell boundaries will be shown on the horizontal (bottom) axis. The resulting histogram is shown in figure 6.3.

Table 6.6-Cell Boundaries

Cell Number	Lower Cell Boundary	Upper Cell Boundary
1	0.9815	0.9855
2	0.9855	0.9895
3	0.9895	0.9935
4	0.9935	0.9975
5	0.9975	1.0015
6	1.0015	1.0055
7	1.0055	1.0095
8	1.0095	1.0135
9	1.0135	1.0175
10	1.0175	1.0215

Pointers for using histograms

● Histograms can be used to compare a process to requirements if you draw the specification lines on the histogram. If you do this, be sure to scale the histogram accordingly.

● Histograms should not be used alone. Always construct a run chart or a control chart before constructing a histogram. Run charts and control charts are described in subsequent chapters. They are needed because histograms will often conceal out of control conditions due to the fact that they don't show the time sequence of the data.

● Evaluate the pattern of the histogram to determine if you can detect changes of any kind. The changes will usually be indicated by multiple modes or "peaks" on the histogram. Most real-world processes produce histograms with a single peak. However, histograms from small samples often have multiple peaks that merely represent sampling

Table 6.7-Frequency Tally Sheet

Cell Number	Cell Start	Cell End	Tally	Frequency
1	0.9815	0.9855	ⅢⅢ	8
2	0.9855	0.9895	ⅢⅢ	9
3	0.9895	0.9935	ⅢⅢⅢ	17
4	0.9935	0.9975	ⅢⅢⅢ	16
5	0.9975	1.0015	ⅢⅢ	9
6	1.0015	1.0055	ⅢⅢⅢⅢ	19
7	1.0055	1.0095	ⅢⅢ	11
8	1.0095	1.0135	ⅢⅠ	6
9	1.0135	1.0175	‖‖	3
10	1.0175	1.0215	‖	2

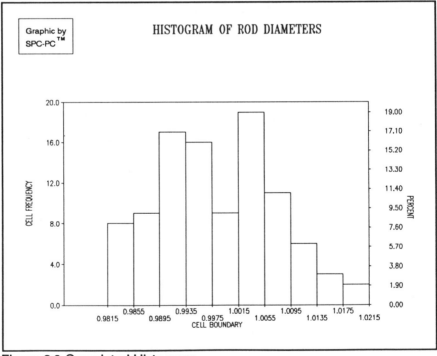

Figure 6.3-Completed Histogram

variation. Also, multiple peaks are sometimes caused by an unfortunate choice of cells.

● Compare histograms from different periods of time. Changes in histogram patterns from one time period to the next can be very useful in finding ways to improve the process.

● Stratify the data by plotting separate histograms for different sources of data. For example, with the rod diameter histogram we might want to plot separate histograms for shafts made from different vendors' materials or made by different operators. This can sometimes reveal things that even control charts don't detect.

Scatter diagrams

Definition   A scatter diagram is a plot of one variable versus another. One variable is called the "independent variable" and it is usually shown on the horizontal (bottom) axis. The other variable is

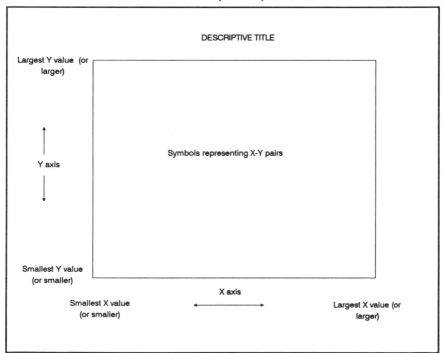

Figure 6.4-Layout of a Scatter Diagram

called the "dependent variable" and it is shown on the vertical (side) axis.

Usage   Scatter diagrams are used to evaluate cause and effect relation-ships. The assumption is that the independent variable is caus-ing a change in the dependent variable. Scatter plots are used to answer such questions as "Does vendor A's material machine better than vendor B's?", "Does the length of training have any-thing to do with the amount of scrap an operator makes?", and so on.

How to construct a scatter diagram

1. Gather several **paired sets** of observations, preferably 20 or more. A

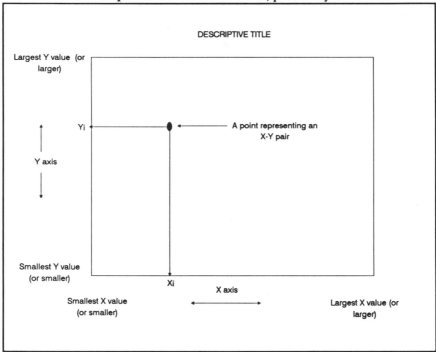

Figure 6.5-How Points Are Plotted on a Scatter Diagram

paired set is one where the dependent variable can be **directly** tied to the independent variable.

2. Find the largest and smallest independent variable and the largest and smallest dependent variable.

3. Construct the vertical and horizontal axes so that the smallest and largest values can be plotted. Figure 6.4 shows the basic structure of a scatter diagram.
4. Plot the data by placing a mark at the point corresponding to each X-Y pair, as illustrated by figure 6.5. If more than one classification is used you may use different symbols to represent each group.

Example of a scatter diagram.

The orchard manager has been keeping track of the weight of peaches on a day by day basis. The data are provided in table 6.8.

Step 1   Organize the data into X-Y pairs, as shown in table 6.8. The independent variable, X, is the number of days the fruit has been

Table 6.8-Raw Data for Scatter Diagram

Number	Days on Tree	Weight (ounces)
1	75	4.5
2	76	4.5
3	77	4.4
4	78	4.6
5	79	5.0
6	80	4.8
7	80	4.9
8	81	5.1
9	82	5.2
10	82	5.2
11	83	5.5
12	84	5.4
13	85	5.5
14	85	5.5
15	86	5.6
16	87	5.7
17	88	5.8
18	89	5.8
19	90	6.0
20	90	6.1

Table 6.9-Smallest and Largest Values

Variable	Smallest	Largest
Days on Tree (X)	75	90
Weight of Peach (Y)	4.4	6.1

on the tree. The dependent variable, Y, is the weight of the peach.

Step 2   Find the largest and smallest values for each data set. The largest and smallest values from table 6.8 are shown in table 6.9.

Step 3   Construct the axes. In this case we need a horizontal axis that allows us to cover the range from 75 to 90 days. The vertical axis must cover the smallest of the small weights (4.4 ounces) to the largest of the weights (6.1 ounces). We will select values beyond

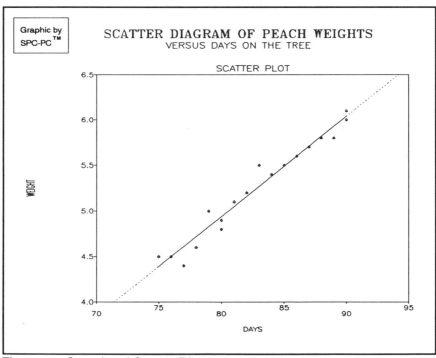

Figure 6.6-Completed Scatter Diagram

these minimum requirements because we want to estimate how long it will take for a peach to reach 6.5 ounces.

Step 4   Plot the data. The completed scatter diagram is shown in figure 6.6.

Pointers for using scatter diagrams

- Scatter diagrams display different patterns that must be interpreted, figure 6.7 provides a scatter diagram interpretation guide.

- Be sure that the independent variable, X, is varied over a sufficiently large range. When X is changed only a small amount you may not see a correlation with Y even though the correlation really does exist.

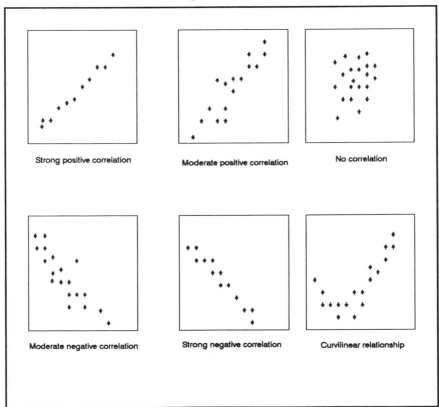

Figure 6.7-Scatter Diagram Interpretation Guidelines

- If you make a prediction for Y for an X value that lies outside of the range you tested be advised that the prediction is highly questionable and should be tested thoroughly. Predicting a Y value beyond the X range actually tested is called **extrapolation**. In figure 6.6 a line has been drawn in to aid predictions. The extrapolation region is shown as a dotted line.

- Keep an eye out for the effect of variables you **didn't** evaluate. Often, an uncontrolled variable will wipe out the effect of your X variable. It is also possible that an uncontrolled variable will be causing the effect and you will mistake the X variable you are controlling as the true cause. This problem is much less likely to occur if you choose X levels at random. An example of this is our peaches. It is possible that any number of variables changed steadily over the time period investigated. It is possible that these variables, and not the independent variable, are responsible for the weight gain (eg, was fertilizer added periodically during the time period investigated?).

- Beware of "happenstance" data! Happenstance data is data that was collected in the past for a purpose different than constructing a scatter diagram. Since little or no control was exercised over important variables, you may find nearly anything. Happenstance data should be used only to get ideas for further investigation, never for reaching final conclusions. One common problem with happenstance data is that the variable that is truly important is not recorded. For example, records might show a correlation between the defect rate and the shift. However, perhaps the real cause of defects is the ambient temperature, which also changes with the shift.

- If there is more than one possible source for the dependent variable, try using different plotting symbols for each source. For example, if the orchard manager knew that some peaches were taken from trees near a busy highway he could use a different symbol for those peaches. He might find an **interaction**, that is, perhaps the peaches from trees near the highway have a different growth rate than those from trees deep within the orchard.

- Although it is possible to do advanced analysis without plotting the scatter diagram, this is generally bad practice. For example, the line in figure 6.6 was fitted using linear regression and the regression analysis can be done without producing the scatter diagram. This misses the enormous learning opportunity provided by the graphical analysis of the data.

CHAPTER 7

RUN CHARTS

Objectives
After completing this section you will:

- Be able to prepare, analyze, and interpret run charts.

- Be able to prepare, analyze, and interpret "pseudo control charts."

Run charts

Definition   Run charts are plots of data arranged in time sequence. Analysis of run charts is performed to determine if the patterns can be attributed to common causes of variation, or if special causes of variation were present.

Usage   Run charts should be used for preliminary analysis of any data measured on a continuous scale that can be organized in time sequence. Run chart candidates include such things as fuel consumption, production throughput, weight, size, etc.. Run charts answer the question "was this process in statistical control for the time period observed?" If the answer is NO, then the process was influenced by one or more special causes of variation. If the answer is YES, then the long-term performance of the process can be estimated.

How to prepare and analyze run charts

1. Plot a line chart of the data in time sequence.
2. Find the median of the data. This can be easily done by using the line chart you constructed in the above step. Simply place a straightedge or a piece of paper across the top of the chart, parallel to the bottom axis. Lower the straightedge until half of the data points appear above the straightedge, or on it. Draw a horizontal line across the chart at that point and label the line "Median" or $\tilde{x}$. This procedure is shown in figure 7.1.

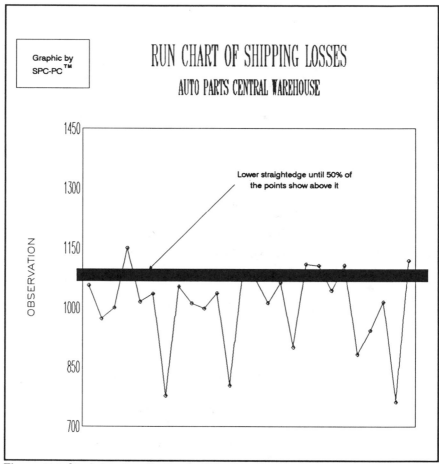

Figure 7.1-Straightedge Method of Finding the Median

As you might expect, run charts are evaluated by examining the "runs" on the chart. A run is a time ordered sequence of points. There are several different statistical tests that can be applied to the runs.

Run length A run to the median is a series of consecutive points on the same side of the median. Unless the process is being influenced by special causes, it is unlikely that a long series of consecutive points will all fall on the same side of the median. Thus, checking run length is one way of checking for special causes of variation. The length of a run is found by simply counting the number of consecutive points on the same side of the median. How-

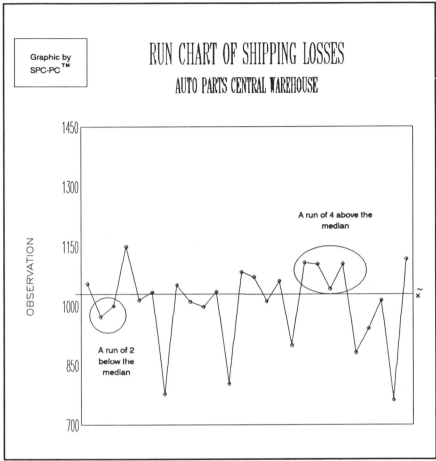

Figure 7.2-Determining Run Length

ever, it may be that some values are **exactly** equal to the median. If only 1 value is exactly on the median line, ignore it [1]. If more than 1 value is on the line, assign them to one side or the other in a way that results in 50% being on one side and 50% on the other. On the run chart, mark those that will be counted as

---

1 There will always be at least one value exactly on the median if you have an odd number of data points

Table 7.1-Maximum Run Length

Number of Values	Maximum Run Length
10	5
15	6
20	7
30	8
40	9
50	10

above the median with an "a" and those that will be counted below the median with a "b." The run length concept is illustrated in figure 7.2.

After finding the longest run, compare the length of the longest run to the values in table 7.1. If the longest run is longer than the maximum allowed, then the process was probably (approximately a 95% probability) influenced by a special cause of variation. With the example there are 26 values plotted and the longest run was 4. Table 7.1 indicates that a run of 7 would not be too unusual for 20 plotted points and a run of 8 would not be too unusual for 30 plotted points. Since we have plotted 26 points we would not investigate a run of 7 but we would investigate a run of 8. Since our longest run is shorter than 8 we conclude that no special cause of variation is indicated and allow the process to continue without investigation. If we had plotted exactly 20 points we would not investigate a run of 7, but we would investigate runs larger than 7.[2]

Number of
runs
The number of runs we expect to find from a controlled process can also be mathematically determined. A process that is not being influenced by special causes will not have either too many runs or too few runs. The number of runs is found by simple counting. Referring to figure 7.3 we see that there are 17 runs.

Table 7.2 is used to evaluate the number of runs. If you have fewer runs than the smallest allowed or more runs than the

---

[2]   Actually, unless the cost of investigating is very high, these "borderline situations" are often worth investigating.

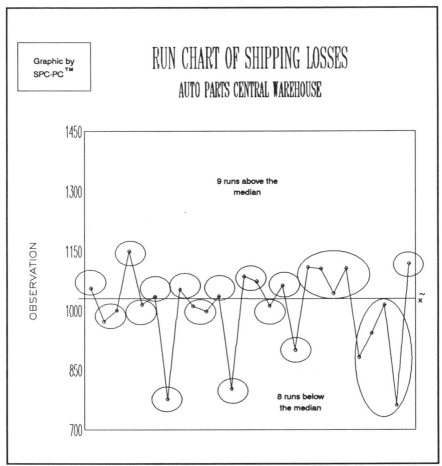

Figure 7.3-Determining the Number of Runs

largest allowed then there is a high probability that a special cause is present. With the example, we have 26 values plotted and 17 runs. Table 7.2 indicates that for 25 or 26 plotted points 9 to 18 runs are normal, so we conclude that no special cause was present.

Trends   The run chart should not have any unusually long series of con-secutive increases or decreases. If it does, then a trend is indi-cated and it is probably due to a special cause of variation. Compare the longest count of consecutive increases or decreases to the longest allowed shown in table 7.3, if your

Table 7.2-Limits on Number of Runs

Number of Values	Smallest Run Count	Largest Run Count
10	3	8
12	3	10
14	4	11
16	5	12
18	6	13
20	6	15
22	7	16
24	8	17
26	9	18
28	10	19
30	11	20
32	11	22
34	12	23
36	13	24
38	14	25
40	15	26
42	16	27
44	17	28
46	17	30
48	18	31
50	19	32

count exceeds the table value then there is a strong probability that a special cause of variation caused your process to drift.

When counting increases or decreases, ignore "no change" values.

Related techniques

Run charts are variables charts. There are many other SPC variables charts including $\bar{x}$ charts, range charts, sigma charts, and individuals control charts. Run charts have two advantages over all of these charts: they are easier to construct, and they are **non-parametric**. A non-parametric statistical method is one that doesn't require any assumptions about the distribution of

Table 7.3-Maximum Consecutive Increases or Decreases

Number of Values	Maximum Consecutive Increases or Decreases
5 to 8	4
9 to 20	5
21 to 100	6
101+	7

the population from which the sample is drawn. Most of the other SPC variables charts require that the population be normally distributed, at least approximately.

Pointers for using run charts.

- Run charts should not be used if too many of the numbers are the same. As a rule of thumb don't use run charts if more than 30% of the values are the same. For example, in the data set 1, 2, 3, 3, 6, 7, 7, 11, 17, 19 the number 3 appears twice and the number 7 appears twice. Thus, 4 of the 10, or 40% of the values are the same.

- Run charts are preliminary analysis tools, if you have continuous data in time-order always sketch a quick run chart before doing any more complex analysis. Often the patterns on a run chart will point you in the right direction without any further work.

- Run charts are one of the least sensitive SPC techniques. They are especially insensitive to "freaks," single points dramatically different from the rest. Thus, run charts may fail to find a special cause even if a special cause was present. In statistical parlance, run charts tend to have large Type II errors, i.e. they have a high probability of accepting the hypothesis of no special cause even when the special cause actually exists. See the following section entitled "Pseudo Control Charts" for a means of detecting freak values. Control charts are more sensitive to freak value than run charts.

- Use run charts to aid in troubleshooting. The different run tests indicate different types of special causes. A long run on the same side of the median indicates a special cause that created a process **shift**. A long series of consecutively increasing or decreasing values indicates a special cause that created a **trend**. Too many runs often indicates

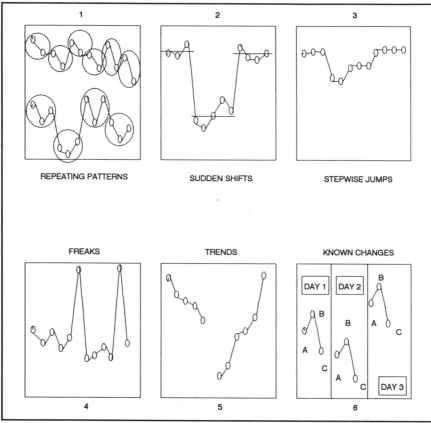

Figure 7.4-Guide for Interpreting Run Chart Patterns

mixture of several sources of variation in the sample. Too few runs often occur in conjunction with a process shift or trend. If you have too few runs and they are not caused by a process shift or trend, then too few runs may indicate **mixture** that follows a definite pattern (eg, an operator who is periodically relieved). Figure 7.4 provides a guide for evaluating some common run chart patterns.

● Chart 1 in figure 7.4 (upper left) illustrates examination of groups. In this case the top line indicates that when the data is examined in groups of two, the second value in the pair is always less than the first value. The bottom line indicates a pattern when examined in groups of three. What could cause these patterns? Look for process features that occur in two's (eg, a two-station fixture) or three's (eg, three shifts).

- Chart 2 shows sudden large shifts followed by periods of relative stability. Try to find out what happened at the change points.

- Chart 3 shows a pattern where certain numbers occur frequently while other numbers seldom or never occur. This pattern often appears because of inadequate gage precision. It also occurs due to rounding, such as an inspector rounding gage readings to the nearest thousandth or half-thousandth.

- Chart 4 shows occasional freak values, separated by periods of relative stability. This may be due to an error in recording the data, inspection error, reacting to an out of specification condition, or over adjusting the process.

- Trends, as indicated by chart 5, are often caused by normal degradation of process inputs. Common examples are tool wear, anode consumption in a plating bath, or consumption of a catalyst in a chemical process.

- Chart 6 shows how patterns often appear when the data is labeled with known process conditions present when the data points were generated. In the example, condition B seems to result in the highest readings, A the next largest, and C seems to result in lower readings than conditions A or B. This seems to hold regardless of the shift.

- The run chart can only suggest possibilities, follow up studies are usually necessary before reaching any conclusions.

Pseudo control charts (optional)

One of the problems with run charts is their inability to determine if "freak values" or outliers are present. An outlier indicates that a special cause of variation was present. A simple and non-parametric method of evaluating outliers is as follows:

1. Find the mean, $\bar{x}$, using equation 5.2.
2. Find the standard deviation, s, using equation 5.4. Many calculators can compute this statistic automatically.
3. Compute the "allowable spread" as

$$Spread = 4 \times s \qquad (7.1)$$

4. Find the lower pseudo control limit and upper pseudo control limit as
$$Pseudo\ Lower\ Control\ Limit = \bar{x} - Spread \qquad (7.2)$$

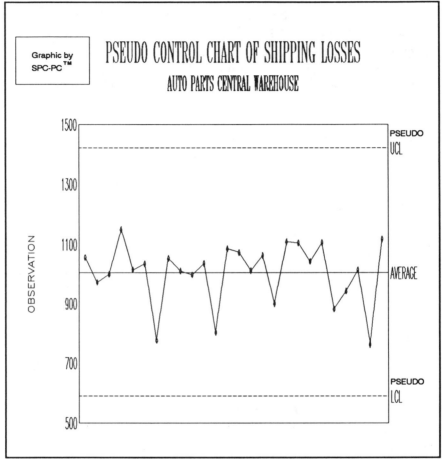

Figure 7.5-Pseudo Control Chart

$$Pseudo\ Upper\ Control\ Limit = \bar{x} + Spread \qquad (7.3)$$

These pseudo control limits are based on methods that do not assume the underlying distribution is normal.[3] If the process distribution is unimodal (ie,

---

3   Shewhart, W.A., Economic Control of Quality of Manufactured Product, ASQC. Milwaukee, Wisconsin, 1980, pp. 176 ff.

the histogram has only one peak) the probability of a single point exceeding a pseudo control limit if the process is in control is no more than approximately 1 in 36.[4] Even for the relatively rare multimodal process distributions (ie, the histogram has more than one peak) the probability of exceeding the pseudo control limit when the process is in control is no more than approximately 1 in 16.[5] If the process distribution is close to normal or if averages can be used, the probabilities of exceeding the pseudo control limits is extremely small and regular control charts, described later in this book, should be used instead. In short, if a value exceeds a pseudo control limit, something probably happened. Figure 7.5 shows the run chart we have been evaluating with pseudo control limits added. The data had an average of $\bar{x}$ = $1005 and a standard deviation s = $104. Thus, Spread = 4 × $104 = $416 and the pseudo control limits are at $1005 ± $416 = $589 and $1421. None of the values fall beyond these limits.

Pointers for Using Pseudo Control Charts

- Although pseudo control limits provide a crude estimate of whether or not an outlier indicates a special cause of variation, the control charts described later in this book provide more powerful tests.

- While control chart usage is nearly universal, pseudo control chart usage is not. Thus, pseudo control charts may not be accepted by customers or management as a legitimate SPC technique. However, the method described here has the advantage of not depending on the underlying distribution of the data. If you need this feature they provide an excellent SPC tool and you might want to spend some time educating your customer or management to the advantages of pseudo control charts.

- Be sure to properly label pseudo control charts so they are not confused with classical control charts. See figure 7.5 for an example. Note that the title and the control limit labels clearly state that the chart is a pseudo control chart. Also note that the average is still the average, and not a "pseudo average."

---

4   Based on the Camp-Meidell inequality,
5   Based on Tchebycheff's inequality.

- Pseudo control chart patterns can be analyzed using figure 7.4, just like run chart patterns. However, the run tests for run length and number of runs described earlier in this chapter will only work with the median, not the average. The trend test, which does not use the median line as a reference, can still be applied and the pseudo control limits provide additional confirmation of "freaks."

CHAPTER 8

AVERAGE, RANGE AND SIGMA CHARTS

Objectives
After completing this section you will:

- Be able to prepare, analyze, and interpret control charts for the average, range, and standard deviation (sigma).

Average, range and sigma charts

Definitions   Average charts are statistical tools used to evaluate the central tendency of a process over time. Range and sigma charts are statistical tools used to evaluate the dispersion or spread of a process over time.

Usage   Average charts answer the question "Has a special cause of variation caused the central tendency of this process to change over the time period observed?" Range or sigma charts answer the question "Has a special cause of variation caused the process distribution to become more or less erratic?"

Range charts or sigma charts are nearly always used in conjunction with another SPC chart that evaluates the central tendency of the process. Most often the other SPC chart is an averages chart, although median charts, moving averages charts, or individuals charts are sometimes used. Average and range or sigma charts can be applied to any continuous variable like weight, size, etc..

How to prepare and analyze $\bar{x}$ and R charts
1. Determine the subgroup size. Typically, subgroups of 4 to 6 units are sufficient and subgroups of 5 are most common. The subgroup size affects the sensitivity of the control chart. Smaller subgroups give a control chart that is less sensitive to changes in the process, while larger sub-

groups are too sensitive to small unimportant changes. Another factor to consider is the central limit theorem, for distributions that are extremely non-normal in shape subgroups of at least 4 are necessary to assure that averages will be approximately normally distributed. Do not use R charts if your subgroup size is larger than 10. In these cases s charts are preferred, see below.

If you have some history, table 8.1 can be used as a guide for determining the subgroup size. To use the table you should determine the size of the average shift that occurs when the $\bar{x}$ chart goes out of control. Then divide the shift by the standard deviation and use this number to enter table 8.1, column 1. The recommended sample size is in column 2. The sample sizes in table 8.1 provide the minimum total inspection required to detect a specified shift. [1]

As an example, assume the process average is 100mm while the process is in control and the standard deviation σ is 10mm. When the process goes out of control the average changes to either 85mm or 115mm, so the average shift is 15mm. Dividing 15mm by $\sigma = 10$mm gives a shift of 1.5σ. Entering table 8.1 we find that a shift of 1.5σ corresponds to a sample size of 5.

2. Determine the sampling frequency. Sampling should be frequent enough to detect the effect of special causes while the special cause itself can still be identified. This varies a great deal from process to process, but as a rule of thumb you should average about 1 out of control point per typical control chart of 25 groups. If you have more than that, increase the sampling frequency. If you have fewer, reduce the sampling frequency.

3. Determine the subgroup selection procedure. Selection of subgroups should be planned to minimize possible variation. This is usually accomplished by selecting consecutive units. Do not deliberately include known sources of variation in the same subgroup. For example, if a machine has several stations your subgroup should not include samples from more than one station. Subgroup selection is crucial to valid use of control charts.

4. Collect data from 25 subgroups, at least 100 individual values are recommended. If your situation does not permit you the luxury of collecting data on 100 individual values, take what you can get and proceed. It is better to use SPC with less data than to stumble along blindly just because you don't have the recommended number of data points. While

---

1   Weiler, H., (1952), "On the Most Economical Sample Size for Controlling the Mean of a Population," Annals of Mathematical Statistics, vol. 23.

Table 8.1-Subgroup Size Determination Guide

Shift in σ Units	Subgroup Size
0.10	1,110
0.20	278
0.30	123
0.40	69
0.50	44
0.60	31
0.70	23
0.80	17
0.90	14
1.00	11
1.10	9
1.20	8
1.30	7
1.40	6
1.50	5
1.60	4
1.70	4
1.80	3
1.90	3
2.00	3
2.10	3
2.20	2
2.30	2
2.40	2
2.50	2
2.60	2
2.70	2
2.80	1
2.90	1
3.00	1

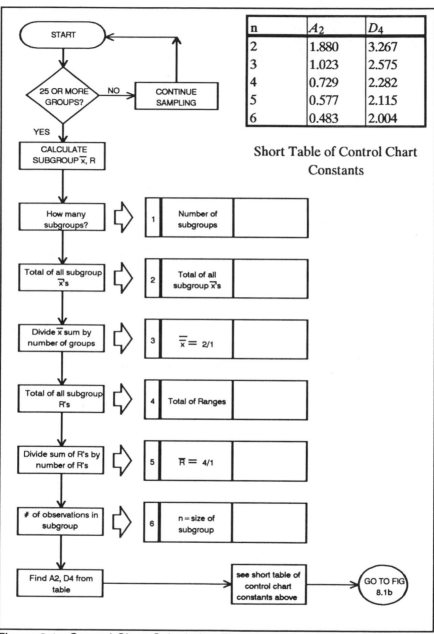

n	A_2	D_4
2	1.880	3.267
3	1.023	2.575
4	0.729	2.282
5	0.577	2.115
6	0.483	2.004

Short Table of Control Chart Constants

Figure 8.1a-Control Chart Calculation Flowchart

86

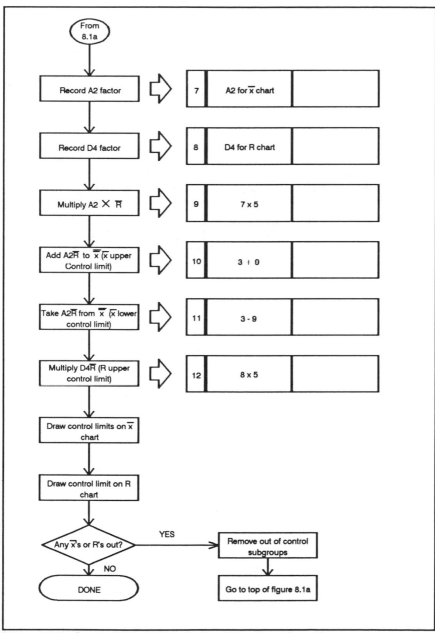

Figure 8.1b-Control Chart Calculation Flowchart (cont.)

the data is being collected, you should minimize disturbances to the process. If a process change is unavoidable, develop a system for recording changes so that their effect can be determined.

5. Perform the necessary calculations. First, for each subgroup separately, compute the average using equation 5.2 and the range using equation 5.3 (see chapter 5). After computing the subgroup averages and ranges, use the flowchart in figures 8.1a and 8.1b to compute the control chart center lines and control limits. The flowchart is based on a flowchart printed in the June 1986 ASQC Statistics Division Newsletter. Each arithmetic instruction in the computational sequence is accompanied by a rectangle divided into three segments: (1) an identification number, (2) a description of the data element or instruction, and (3) a blank space for recording the resultant data. Numbers written beneath the description or instruction in segment (2) refer you back to the rectangles corresponding. In the descriptive portion of rectangle number 5

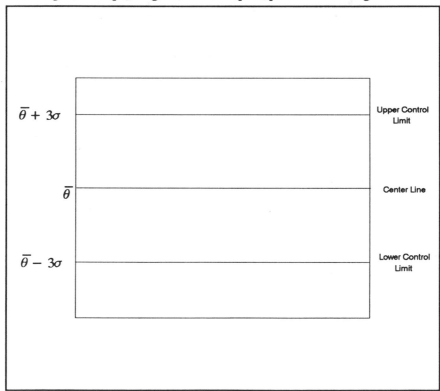

Figure 8.2-Layout of All Classical Control Charts

for example, **4/1** means that you should divide the data element written in rectangle number 4 by the data element in rectangle 1. By stepping through this simple logic, you will calculate control limits for both $\bar{x}$ and R charts by the time you complete the flow chart.

All classical control charts have a center line, the average, and control limits at three sigma on each side of the average. The layout of all control charts is illustrated in figure 8.2. The "performance measure" can be any of a variety of statistics, including the subgroup average, range, standard deviation, number defective, defects per 100 units, etc.. If the statistic is bounded at some value the control limit may not exist. For example, the subgroup range is bounded by 0 and for sample sizes of 6 or less and there is no lower control limit for the range. Likewise, a control chart for percent defective is

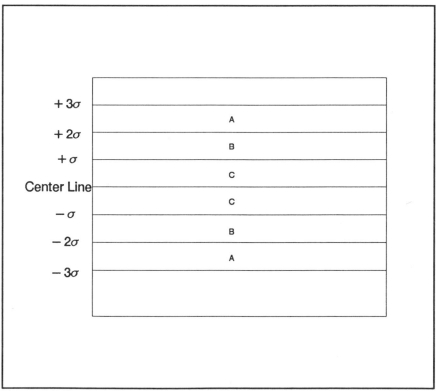

Figure 8.3-Control Chart Divided Into Zones

bounded at 0% and 100% and the control limits will not exist if they are larger beyond these bounds.

Interpretation of control charts

The interpretation of control charts for the average and the range involve two considerations: freaks and non-random patterns. Either situation represents the presence of a special cause of variation, as described in chapter 5. Freaks are detected by comparing each individual subgroup average and range to the control limits computed in rectangles 10, 11, and 12 in the figure 8.1 flowcharts. The upper control limit for the averages is the value in rectangle 10, the lower control limit for the averages is the value in rectangle 11. The upper control limit for the ranges is given in rectangle 12, for subgroups of less than 7 the lower control limit for the ranges is 0. When the process distribution is in statistical control the probability of exceeding a control limit is very small. Thus, when an average or range exceeds a control limit a special cause of variation can probably be identified. In other words,

Control Charts Are An Operational Definition Of A Special Cause. They Are Not a Statistical Test of Hypothesis.

In addition to looking for points beyond the control limits, the patterns on the control chart can also be evaluated to determine if special causes exist. This is done in much the same way as we analyzed patterns on run charts (in fact, if you review the definition in chapter 7 you will see that averages and ranges control charts **are** run charts!). However, with run charts we assumed nothing about the distribution and our tests were therefore less sensitive to process changes than $\bar{x}$ and R charts. Because of the central limit theorem, with averages charts we are usually safe to assume that the normal distribution is approximately correct. Using this assumption we can design a series of much more sensitive run tests. To do this we divide the zone between the two control limits into six equal parts. This divides each half of the control chart into 3 zones. The 3 zones are labeled A, B, and C as shown in figure 8.3.

Using figure 8.3 we can apply tests for non-random patterns and runs. Remember, the existence of a non-random pattern means that a special cause of variation was (or is) probably present. Since the distribution is as-

sumed to be normal, the runs test we will apply are different than those we used for run charts. Our $\bar{x}$ control chart tests are shown in figure 8.4. [2]
The patterns on the control charts can be used as an aid in troubleshooting. See figure 7.4 in the previous chapter for a run chart troubleshooting guide.

Example

Recall that we prepared a histogram of peach weights. Since the data were collected in subgroups of 5, the data that was used for preparing our his-

Table 8.2-Data for Control Charts

Row	No. 1	No. 2	No. 3	No. 4	No. 5	$\bar{x}$	R
1	1.002	0.995	1.000	1.002	1.005	1.0008	0.010
2	1.000	0.997	1.007	0.992	0.995	0.9982	0.015
3	0.997	1.013	1.001	0.985	1.002	0.9996	0.028
4	0.990	1.008	1.005	0.994	1.012	1.0018	0.022
5	0.992	1.012	1.005	0.985	1.006	1.0000	0.027
6	1.000	1.002	1.006	1.007	0.993	1.0016	0.014
7	0.984	0.994	0.998	1.006	1.002	0.9968	0.022
8	0.987	0.994	1.002	0.997	1.008	0.9976	0.021
9	0.992	0.988	1.015	0.987	1.006	0.9976	0.028
10	0.994	0.990	0.991	1.002	0.988	0.9930	0.014
11	1.007	1.008	0.990	1.001	0.999	1.0010	0.018
12	0.995	0.989	0.982	0.995	1.002	0.9926	0.020
13	0.987	1.004	0.992	1.002	0.992	0.9954	0.017
14	0.991	1.001	0.996	0.997	0.984	0.9938	0.017
15	1.004	0.993	1.003	0.992	1.010	1.0004	0.018
16	1.004	1.010	0.984	0.997	1.008	1.0006	0.026
17	0.990	1.021	0.995	0.987	0.989	0.9964	0.034
18	1.003	0.992	0.992	0.990	1.014	0.9982	0.024
19	1.000	0.985	1.019	1.002	0.986	0.9984	0.034
20	0.996	0.984	1.005	1.016	1.012	1.0026	0.032

[2]   Nelson, L.S., (1986). "The Shewhart Control Chart - Tests for Special Causes," Journal of Quality Technology, Vol. 16, No. 4, pp 237-239.

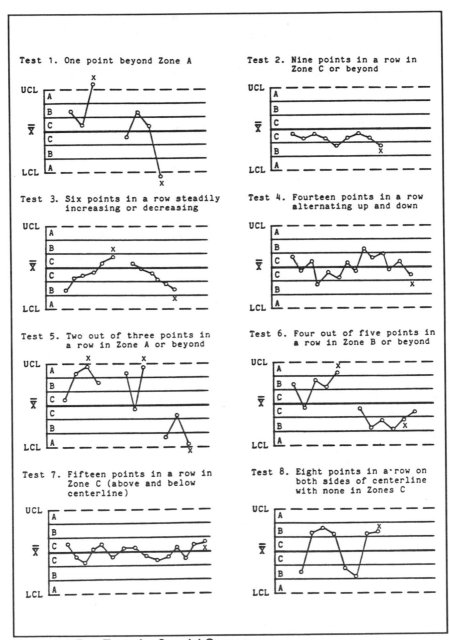

Figure 8.4-Run Tests for Special Causes

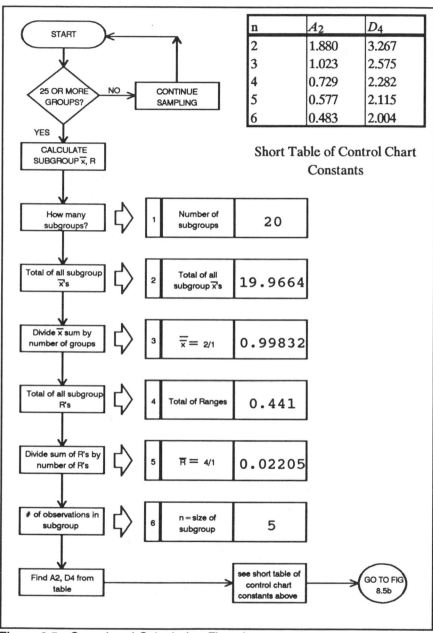

n	A_2	D_4
2	1.880	3.267
3	1.023	2.575
4	0.729	2.282
5	0.577	2.115
6	0.483	2.004

Short Table of Control Chart Constants

Figure 8.5a-Completed Calculation Flowchart

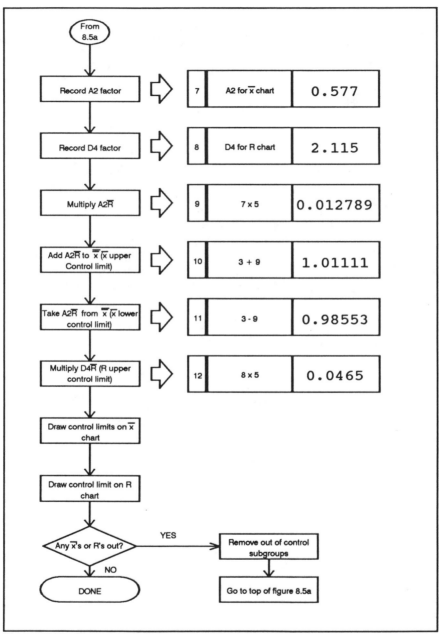

Figure 8.5b-Completed Calculation Flowchart (cont.)

togram can also be analyzed using averages and ranges control charts. The average and range in the table are computed using equations 5.2 and 5.3 respectively, which are repeated below

$$\bar{x} = \frac{1}{n} \sum_{i=1}^{n} x_i$$

(equation 5.2 repeated)

$$R = Largest - Smallest$$

(equation 5.3 repeated)

The raw data with subgroup averages and ranges are shown in table 8.2. The data in table 8.2 is used to complete the worksheet from figures 8.1a and 8.1b. The completed worksheets are shown in figures 8.5a and 8.5b. Note that when completing the form for rectangles 10 and 11 we carried two more decimal places than the raw data contain. We recommend the average be rounded to one decimal place more than the raw data. The range control limit in rectangle 12 has one more decimal place than the raw data. The above conventions eliminate the ambiguity that might result if a sample average or range fell exactly on the control limit. The completed control charts are shown in figure 8.6. The process appears to be in control. In addition to the 3 sigma control limits we will also analyze the patterns. The charts in figure 8.7 show zones A, B, and C lines on the charts. The averages $(\bar{x})$ chart is in control by all 8 tests for non-randomness. So is the range chart. You might have noticed that the range chart zones aren't ex- actly right. The zones on both charts were obtained by simply dividing the distance between the upper and lower control limits by 6. This worked per- fectly for the averages chart, but you can see the average range line is slightly **below** the 3rd line instead of exactly on it. This is because the distribution of the range of subgroups of 4 or larger is only **approximately** normal. How- ever, it is close enough to apply the run tests without change. This is **not** true for subgroups of 2 or 3. For subgroups of 2 or 3 apply the run tests described in chapter 7, using the median instead of the average range.

Sigma charts (s charts)

S charts provide essentially the same information as range charts, namely, they answer the question "has a special cause of variation caused the process distribution to become more erratic?" However, s charts are statistically more efficient than range charts in the sense that an increase in the process

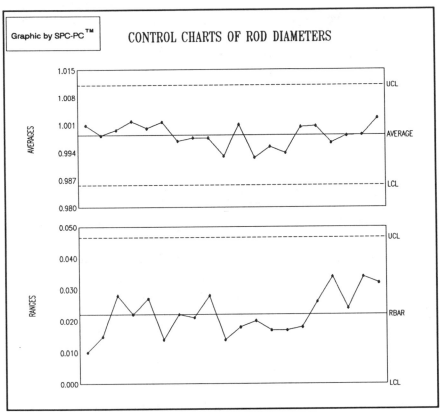

Figure 8.6-Control Charts for Average and Range

spread is more likely to be detected in a sample of a given size using sigma charts than using range charts. The advantage of s charts over R charts increases as the subgroup size increases. In fact, R charts are so inefficient for large subgroup sizes that they should not be used if the group size is larger than 10.

S charts are created in almost exactly the same way as R charts. Like R charts, s charts are usually kept along with average charts. The procedure for completing $\bar{x}$ and s charts is the same as that described earlier in this chapter in the section entitled "How to prepare and analyze $\bar{x}$ and R charts." There are two major differences:

1. The subgroup standard deviations are used to measure the process spread instead of the subgroup ranges. The subgroup standard devia-

tions are computed separately for each subgroup using formula 5.4, which is repeated here

$$s = \sqrt{\sum_{i=1}^{n} \frac{(x_i - \overline{x})^2}{n-1}}$$

(equation 5.4 repeated)

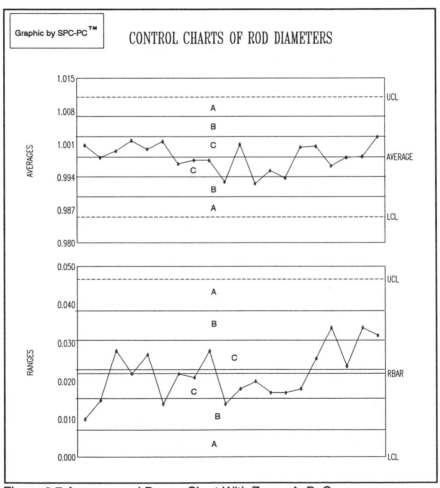

Figure 8.7-Average and Range Chart With Zones A, B, C

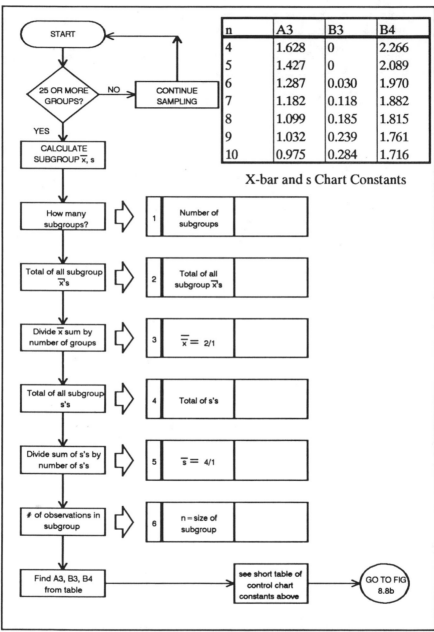

n	A3	B3	B4
4	1.628	0	2.266
5	1.427	0	2.089
6	1.287	0.030	1.970
7	1.182	0.118	1.882
8	1.099	0.185	1.815
9	1.032	0.239	1.761
10	0.975	0.284	1.716

X-bar and s Chart Constants

Figure 8.8a-XBAR and s Chart Calculation Flowchart

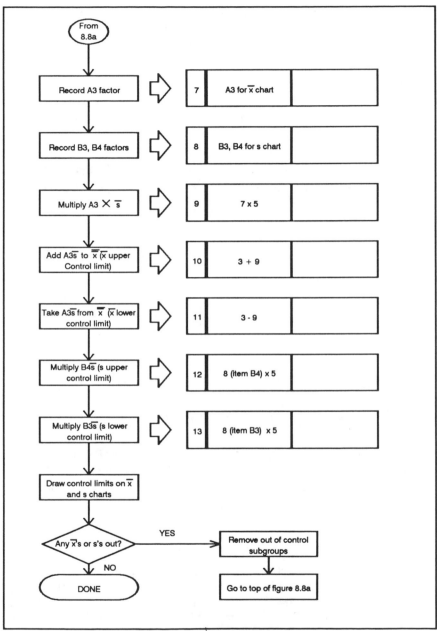

Figure 8.8b-XBAR and s Chart Calculation Flowchart (cont)

2. The control chart center lines and control limits are found using the flowcharts in figures 8.8a and 8.8b. The $\bar{x}$ and s charts are interpreted in exactly the same way as described above for $\bar{x}$ and R charts.

Related techniques

$\bar{x}$ charts are charts of continuous variables. At times it may be appropriate to substitute run charts, individuals charts, median charts, cumulative sum charts, or moving average charts. This series contains information on these other charts.

Moving average charts can be constructed by regrouping the data and performing regular $\bar{x}$ and R chart analysis on the regrouped data. For example, if you have the data 15, 12, 13, 10, 9, 12 and 11 and you want to prepare a

Table 8.3-Groups for Moving Average Charts

Group Number	Data
1	15, 12, 13
2	12, 13, 10
3	13, 10, 9
4	10, 9, 12
5	9, 12, 11

moving average chart with groups of size 3 you would have the groups shown in table 8.3.

Because of the way the groups are formed, you can not use the run tests to analyze patterns on moving average charts. In fact, moving average charts give patterns that are notoriously misleading. As a rule, if the moving average is within the control limits, it is okay.

Pointers for using $\bar{x}$, R, and s charts

- **BE TIMELY!** These charts are tools to assist you with process improvement by highlighting the existence of special causes. It does very little good to know that a special cause was present yesterday - you must know that it is happening **now**. Unless you are timely you will never be able to identify the special cause, it will be a "ghost." To assist you in finding ghosts, frequent small samples are generally better than occasional large samples.

- Always evaluate the s or R chart before looking at the $\bar{x}$ chart. The control limits for the $\bar{x}$ chart are based on either $\bar{R}$ or $\bar{s}$, thus the $\bar{x}$ chart's control limits are meaningless unless the s or R chart show control.

- Log in as much background information as possible. The background data will be very helpful in analyzing patterns that would otherwise seem random. For example, one operator of a lathe noticed that cold air blasted in a door every time a new load of material came in and he noted this fact on his control chart. After a few days it was clear that this caused variation in the size of the parts being made on the lathe. However, this discovery would never have been made without the operator's diligence.

- Write comments on the chart form itself. The most useful control charts are usually not the cleanest ones, they're the ones that have been used!

- Be an "active investigator." Using control charts to "study history" will only get you half of their potential benefit. If you deliberately try different things, and note these things on the charts, you will greatly accelerate the learning process. For example, if you have materials from 2 different sources, why not group one vendor's material together for several subgroups and the other vendor's material for several more, making a note of this on the control charts. If there is a difference, you've uncovered a special cause and you can make an immediate improvement!

- Use R charts unless you have a computer. Although s charts have certain mathematical advantages over R charts, they are not as intuitive as R charts. People can easily relate to the fact that an increase in the range indicates an increase in the process spread. Also, it is much easier to make an error in computing sigma and it is much more difficult to detect the error. Using a calculator doesn't seem to help. I've seen many more errors made with calculators than by hand, and they are more likely to be overlooked since people trust calculators implicitly.

- When a point is out of control, check the easiest things first. The first step is to double check the arithmetic. Next assure that the point is plotted where it should be plotted. There should be a written procedure or flow chart describing the steps to be taken when an s, R, or $\bar{x}$ falls beyond a control limit. The procedure should also describe the action to be taken if the special cause can't be found.

CHAPTER 9

CONTROL CHARTS FOR INDIVIDUALS

Objectives
After completing this section you will:

- Be able to prepare, analyze, and interpret control charts for individuals.
- Know when to use these charts.
- Understand the advantages and disadvantages of these charts.

Control charts for individual values

Definition   *Individuals control charts* are statistical tools used to evaluate the central tendency of a process over time. They are sometimes also called "moving range charts" because of the way in which the control limits are calculated.

Usage   *Individuals control charts* are used when it is not feasible to use averages for process control. There are many possible reasons why averages control charts may not be desireable; observations may be expensive to get (e.g., destructive testing), output may be too homogenous over short time intervals (e.g., pH of a solution), the production rate may be slow and the interval between successive observations long, etc.. Control charts for individuals are often used to monitor batch process, such as chemical processes, where the within batch variation is so small relative to between batch variation that the control limits on a standard $\bar{x}$ chart would be too close together and most $\bar{x}$'s would be out of control. Range charts are used in conjunction with individuals charts to help control dispersion. Individuals charts answer the question "Has a special cause of variation influenced this process?"

How to prepare and analyze individuals charts

1. Determine the sampling frequency. Sampling should be frequent enough to detect the effect of special causes while the special cause itself can still be identified. This varies a great deal from process to process, but as a crude rule of thumb you should average about 1 out of control point per typical control chart of 25 samples. If you have more than that, increase the sampling frequency. If you have fewer, reduce the sampling frequency.

2. Gather observations from the process in time sequence (the more, the better). Initially, the observations should be taken over a short time interval, consecutive units if possible. Arrange the data in a table and find the difference between consecutive values as shown in table 9.1. Note that the **absolute value** of the difference is used. That is, the smaller of any 2 adjacent values is always subtracted from the larger value. As mentioned above, because of the way this is done, this type of control chart is often called a **moving range chart**.

3. Compute the average of all the data and the average of the ranges column. With the data above we obtain

$$\bar{x} = \frac{1}{n} \sum_{i=1}^{n} x_i = \frac{201.4}{30} = 6.713\%$$

$$Moving\ \bar{R} = \frac{1}{n-1} \sum_{i=1}^{n-1} R_i = \frac{23.6}{29} = 0.81\% \tag{9.1}$$

Observe that we have one less range than we have data values because we can't get a range until we have 2 observations.

4. Compute the control limits using the equations below

$$UCL_R = 3.267\bar{R} \tag{9.2}$$

$$LCL_x = \bar{x} - 2.66\bar{R} \tag{9.3}$$

$$UCL_x = \bar{x} + 2.66\bar{R} \tag{9.4}$$

Table 9.1-USA Savings Rate Statistics

Year	Savings Rate	Moving Range
1960	5.8	Can't get on first sample
1961	6.6	0.8
1962	6.5	0.1
1963	5.9	0.6
1964	7.0	1.1
1965	7.0	0.0
1966	6.8	0.2
1967	8.0	1.2
1968	7.0	1.0
1969	6.4	0.6
1970	8.1	1.7
1971	8.5	0.4
1972	7.3	1.2
1973	9.4*	2.1
1974	9.3*	0.1
1975	9.2*	0.1
1976	7.6	1.6
1977	6.6	1.0
1978	7.1	0.5
1979	6.8	0.3
1980	7.1	0.3
1981	7.5	0.4
1982	6.8	0.7
1983	5.4	1.4
1984	6.1	0.7
1985	4.4*	1.7
1986	4.0*	0.4
1987	3.2*	0.8
1988	4.2*	1.0
First quarter 1989	5.8	1.6

The 2.66 is not a new "magic number." The limits are still 3σ from the mean just as before. The constant 2.66 compensates for the fact that

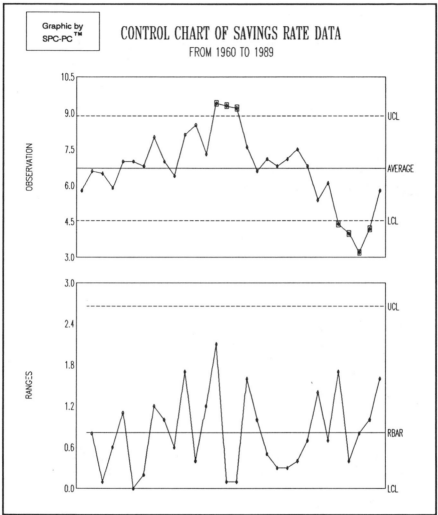

Figure 9.1-Individuals and Moving Range Control Charts

we are measuring dispersion with $\overline{R}$ and not σ. For the data in table 9.1 we get

$$UCL_R = 2.66\%$$

$$LCL_x = 4.55\%$$

$$UCL_x = 8.88\%$$

5. As with $\bar{x}$ charts, the analysis begins with an evaluation of the range chart. Check the moving range column for any values that exceed UCL_R. Drop these ranges and recalculate with those ranges that remain; of course, you must also find the reason for the out-of-control data and eliminate it.

6. Check the raw data for any values that are less than LCL_x or greater than UCL_x. Drop these values and recalculate with those values that remain; as before, you should also find the reason for the out-of-control data and eliminate it.

7. Plot the raw data on the x chart using the upper and lower control limits. The average should be shown as a solid line on the chart and the control limits should be shown as dashed lines. Mark any out-of-control points with a large "X" or by drawing a box around it. Plot the ranges on an R chart as in the previous chapter. The control charts for our sample data is shown in figure 9.1.

8. Analyze runs using the same tests as described in chapter 8 for averages control charts. Using our example, the zones are shown in figure 9.2. Note that run tests are not applied to the R chart when using moving ranges.

9. If you wish, you can use the worksheets in figures 8.1a and 8.1b to compute the parameters for your individuals control charts. Since you are plotting individual values your subgroup size is 1, and the A_2 value is 2.66. The range is based on subgroups of two (consecutive pairs) so D_4 is, from the table in the worksheet, 3.267.

10. With the R chart in control we can estimate the standard deviation as

$$\hat{\sigma} = \frac{\bar{R}}{d_2} \tag{9.5}$$

Where d_2 is a table constant, 1.128 for moving range charts. This estimate of sigma turns out to have a number of advantages over equation 5.4, the "standard" method of computing the standard deviation. One big advantage is that it is less influenced by special causes of variation. For example, if trends were present in the data, as they are with our example, this estimate of sigma will tend to "ride the trend." Equation 5.4, on the other hand, will include variation from the trends and other special causes as well as normal process variation. Thus, using equation 9.5 we estimate $\hat{\sigma} = 0.72\%$ but using equation 5.4 we get $\sigma = 1.50\%$, more than double. With the wider control limits that would result from using equation 5.4 we would miss the out of control conditions completely. These two estimates will be very close if the process is in statistical control.

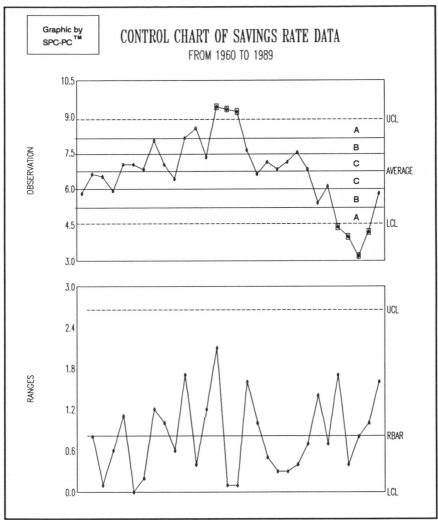

Figure 9.2-Individuals Charts with Zones

Discussion of example

First of all, observe that the range chart shows statistical control. Thus we are justified in evaluating the control chart for the savings rate. If the range chart was not in statistical control it would've indicated a process distribution that was changing drastically in the short term and we would look for special causes that might have this effect.

The example shows that the savings rate "process" was influenced by special causes of variation during two periods of time: 1973 to 1975, when savings were higher than normal, and 1985 to 1988, when savings were lower than normal. The people concerned with this process, government officials, bureaucrats, and economists, etc. need to consider the possible special causes. There are many. Cause and effect diagrams would be helpful in organizing the special causes, as well as the common causes. It is interesting to note that the newspaper article that presented these data never even mentioned the higher than normal savings rate of 1973 - 1975. The discussion focused entirely on the "savings crisis" represented by the more recent out of control condition. Also not mentioned in the analysis was whether or not the average savings rate of the in-control years, roughly 6.9%, would be acceptable.

This example illustrates the problem with such glib advice as "eliminate the special cause of variation." In the real world, it's not always so easy! Nevertheless, the concepts of special causes and common causes are still vital to helping decide the appropriate course of action. With the example, there are two problems to deal with: the current low savings rate, and the long-term savings rate. "Fixing" the cause of the current low savings rate will bring the average back to the historic level. The question is how to improve from there? Again, SPC concepts can help. Perhaps studying the causes of the higher than normal savings rates in 1973 to 1975 can provide valuable clues. Note that for this example we did not drop the 7 out of control groups and recalculate, as we would have under normal circumstances. You may wish to do this as an exercise. The revised center lines and control limits you obtain should be (rounded)

$$\bar{R} = 0.81\%$$
$$UCL_R = 2.66\%$$
$$\bar{x} = 6.86\%$$
$$LCL_x = 4.69\%$$
$$UCL_x = 9.02\%$$

All remaining savings rates and moving ranges will be within these control limits.

Related techniques

X charts are charts of continuous variables. At times it may be appropriate to substitute run charts, $\bar{x}$ and R charts, median charts, cumulative sum charts, or moving average charts. The sensitivity of the chart will be increased by using averages, see chapter 8, table 8.1.

When special causes are present, data collection sheets, histograms, brainstorming and cause and effect diagrams will prove useful in finding them. These same tools will prove helpful in preparing process improvement plans whether the process is in statistical control or not.

Pointers for using X charts

- The same pointers apply here as for $\bar{x}$ and R charts. Reread that section of chapter 8.

- Individuals control charts are based on the assumption that the underlying population is normally distributed, at least approximately. Use a histogram (see chapter 6) or probability paper (see chapter 12) to verify that this is the case. Be aware that people often make too much of the importance of assuming a normal distribution. In practice, these charts usually perform satisfactorily even with non-normal distributions as long as there is a relatively small probability that a single point will exceed 3 standard deviations from the mean when the process is in control. If this is not the case, pseudo control charts can be used instead, see chapter 7 for details.

- Unlike the control limit test for special causes, the run tests *are* sensitive to the assumption of normality. When faced with non-normal distributions you should apply the run tests described in chapter 7 for run charts instead of those described for $\bar{x}$ charts. Of course, the run tests in chapter 7 use the median instead of the average.

CHAPTER 10

CONTROL CHARTS FOR ATTRIBUTES

Objectives
After completing this section you will:

- Be able to prepare, analyze, and interpret control charts for proportion defective (p charts).

- Be able to prepare, analyze, and interpret control charts for number defective (np charts).

- Be able to prepare, analyze, and interpret control charts for defects when the sample size is constant (c charts).

- Be able to prepare, analyze, and interpret control charts for defects when the sample size varies (u charts).

- Understand the difference between variable and attributes performance measures.

Introduction

This section describes control charts for *attribute data*. Attribute data are used to measure the performance of processes by *counting*. Typically the things being counted are flaws or non-conformances, such as typographical errors or errors on invoices. It is also common to count the units that possess the flaws or non-conformances, such as memos with typographical errors or invoices with errors.

Unlike variables performance measures which are measured on continuous scales and can take on any value, attribute performance measures are *discrete* and they can only take on certain values. For example, if the performance measure is the number of invoices in a sample of 100 that have one or more errors, the performance measure can only be one of the whole numbers from

Table 10.1-Attribute Charts and Their Usage

Attribute Chart	Usage
np chart	Control of performance measures that involve unit counts. Usually the units counted possess some attribute, such as a flaw or an error. The subgroup size must be constant. Examples: sample 100 invoices each week and tally the number of invoices with errors; check 50 drilled holes each hour with a go/not-go gage and tally the number of holes that fail the test.
p chart	Same as np charts except that proportions are used instead of the actual counts and sample sizes can vary.
c chart	Control of performance measures that involve occurrence per unit counts. The unit can be a number of items, a time period, or any opportunity for the occurrence to appear. The number of units per subgroup must be constant. Examples: accidents per 100,000 labor hours; defects per square yard of carpet; pieces made per tool; machine breakdowns per day.
u chart	Same as c charts except the number of units per subgroup can vary. The number plotted is the number of occurrences divided by the number of units in the subgroup.

0 to 100. Attribute performance measures can also be monitored with control charts. However, the equations used to compute the chart center lines and control limits are different than those for variables charts. This chapter describes four SPC charts for attributes. A guide to the attribute charts and their usage is provided in table 10.1

The four different charts are quite similar to one another in a number of ways. However, it will be easier to apply the techniques in this chapter if each chart is treated separately. Thus, each chart is described in its own separate section of this chapter. Because of this approach there is a certain amount of duplicated material between the different sections.

Terminology

In an effort to avoid confusion, this chapter is written using the conventional notation for the four attribute control charts, namely the "defect-defective" notation. However, the charts described here can be applied to a much greater variety of process data than merely defect counts or defective unit counts. A brief list of examples of synonyms follows.

Defect   Any *occurrence*, such as parts produced per tool, machine break downs per shift, lost time accidents per unit of time, typographical errors per 1000 written pages, copier breakdowns per 1000 copies, sales per 100 leads, telephone calls per day, etc.. The key to distinguishing a defect from a defective is that a defect is an *occurrence* that can occur multiple times per unit.

Defective   The result of classifying items into one of two discrete categories. A defective is merely the count of items in one of the categories. For example, above we said that sales per 100 leads involved a synonym of the term "defect," sales. Obviously it is possible to have more than one sale for a given lead. However, if we counted leads that resulted in one or more sales we would have a synonym for defective. We have classified sales leads into two categories, sold or not sold, and counted the number in one of the categories. Other examples include invoices with errors, invoices paid late, orders shipped on time, orders shipped complete, project tasks completed by their deadline dates, etc..

np charts for number defective

Definition   np charts are statistical tools used to evaluate the number of defectives produced by a process.

Usage   np charts can be applied to any variable where the sample size is constant and the appropriate performance measure is a unit count. np charts answer the question "Has a special cause of variation caused this process to produce an abnormally large or small number of defective units over the time period observed?"

How to prepare and analyze np charts

1. Determine the subgroup size, rational subgroup, and sampling frequency. The subgroup size **must be constant for all subgroups** and should be large enough that the chart of number of defective in the sample produces a pattern that can be analyzed. A crude rule of thumb is that the average proportion defective multiplied by the subgroup size should be 5 or more. The average proportion defective is found by

$$\bar{p} = \frac{number\ defective}{number\ inspected} \tag{10.1}$$

   Using this rule the sample size would be

$$n \geq \frac{5}{\bar{p}} \tag{10.2}$$

   Sampling should be frequent enough to detect the effect of special causes while the special cause itself can still be identified. This varies a great deal from process to process, but as a crude rule of thumb you should average about 1 out of control point per typical control chart of 25 groups. If you have more than that, increase the sampling frequency. If you have fewer, reduce the sampling frequency.

2. Collect data from 25 subgroups. While the data is being collected, you should minimize disturbances to the process. If a process change is unavoidable, develop a system for recording changes so that their effect can be determined.

3. Establish the control limits. Perform the necessary calculations. The flow chart in figure 10.1 provides a guide for doing the calculations.[1] Each arithmetic instruction in the flowchart's computational sequence is accompanied by rectangles divided into three segments: (1) an identification number, (2) a description of the data element or instruction, and (3) a blank space for recording the resultant data. Numbers written

---

1   Adapted from a flow chart in ASQC Statistics Division Newsletter, June 1986

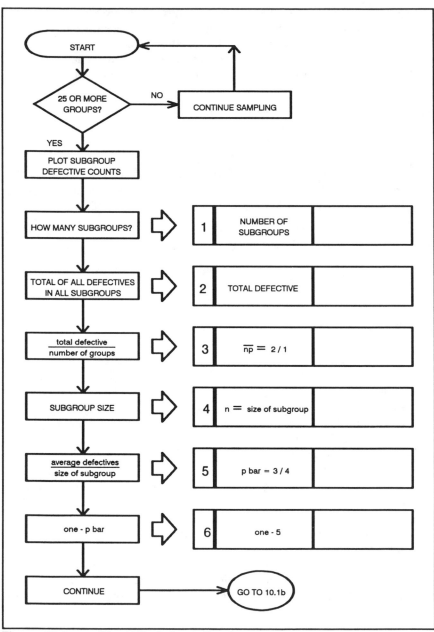

Figure 10.1a-np Chart Worksheet, Part I

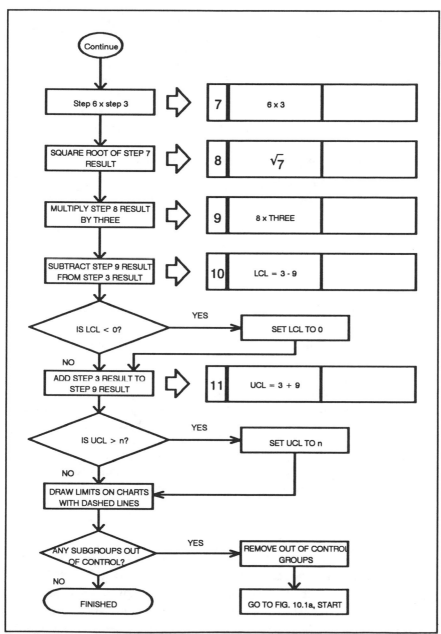

Figure 10.1b-np Chart Worksheet, Part II

beneath the description or instruction in segment (2) refer you back to the rectangles corresponding. In the descriptive portion of rectangle number 3 for example, **2/1** means that you should divide the data element written in rectangle number 2 by the data element in rectangle number 1. By stepping through this sin.ple logic, you will calculate control limits for the np chart by the time you complete the worksheet. To distinguish values from rectangle numbers, when we want you to actually use a numeric value, we will spell out the values we want you to use e.g., three x four = twelve.

The equations being solved with the flowchart are

$$\overline{np} = \frac{total\ number\ defective}{number\ of\ subgroups} \tag{10.3}$$

$$LCL_{np} = \overline{np} - 3\sqrt{\overline{np}\ (1\text{-}\overline{p})} \tag{10.4}$$

$$UCL_{np} = \overline{np} + 3\sqrt{\overline{np}\ (1\text{-}\overline{p})} \tag{10.5}$$

where $\overline{p}$ is computed as shown in equation 10.1 using all the subgroups combined.

4. Analysis of np charts. As with all control charts, a special cause is probably present if there are any points beyond either the lower control limit or the upper control limit. Analysis of np chart patterns between the control limits is complicated by the fact that the distribution of the number defective follows the binomial distribution, not the normal distribution. However, if there is both a lower control limit and an upper control limit the pattern is usually close enough to normal to apply the run tests described for $\overline{x}$ charts in chapter 8.

np chart example

Bob, our friendly neighborhood produce manager, has kept track of the number of bruised peaches in recent shipments. The data in table 10.2 were obtained by opening one randomly selected crate per shipment and counting the number of bruised peaches. There are 250 peaches per crate. Since the number of crates and the number of peaches per crate is the same each time, the sample size is also constant and np charts are appropriate.

Table 10.2-Raw Data for np Chart

Shipment Number	Bruised Peaches
1	20
2	28
3	24
4	21
5	32
6	33
7	31
8	29
9	30
10	34
11	32
12	24
13	29
14	27
15	37
16	23
17	27
18	28
19	31
20	27
21	30
22	23
23	23
24	27
25	35
26	29
27	23
28	23
29	30
30	28

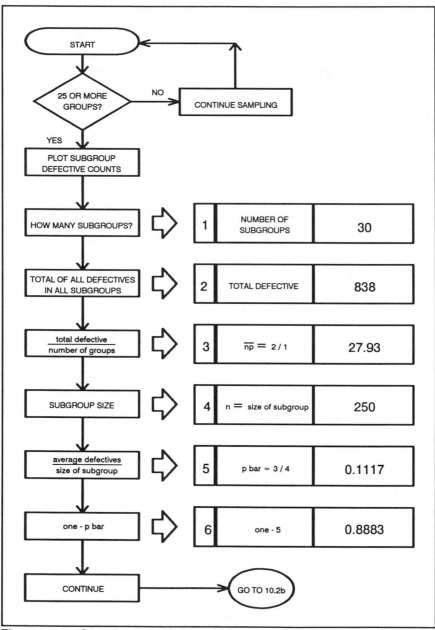

Figure 10.2a-Completed np Chart Worksheet

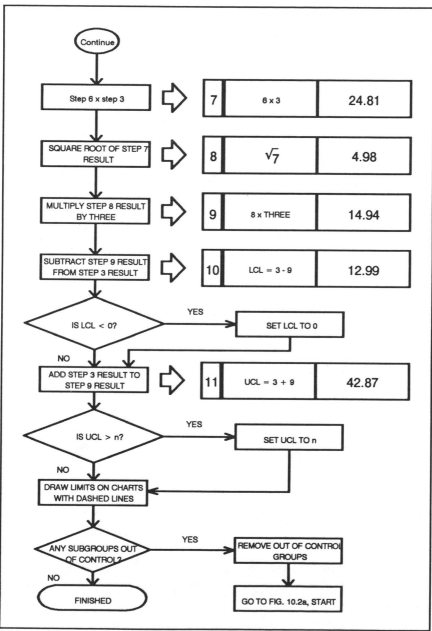

Figure 10.2b-Completed np Chart Worksheet Part II

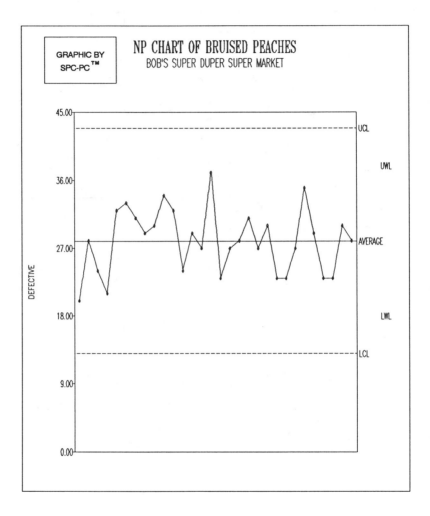

Figure 10.3-Completed np Chart

The data in table 10.2 are used to complete the worksheets from figure 10.1. The completed worksheets are shown in figure 10.2 and the completed np control chart is shown in figure 10.3.

Related techniques

np control charts are used for process control of the number defective when the sample size is constant. p control charts are used when the sample size varies. If the control measure is the number of **defects** instead of the number of defectives (a defective is a **unit** with one or more defects), then a c chart or a u chart is used.

Pointers for using np charts

- Use careful judgement to determine the sample size and the subgroup. For instance, with our example the produce manager used a crate as the subgroup - quite logical. Peaches within a single crate should be relatively homogenous. The subgroup may be 50 consecutive units sampled at a randomly selected time of day, or a full box, or a full pallet.

- Keep a detailed log of the conditions that created a particular subgroup. Which vendor's materials were used? Who was the operator? The inspector? Use the information to investigate patterns, are all of the peak defective counts coming from the same vendor or operator?

- Keep the chart near the operation being charted. Control charts are feedback mechanisms that can't work if they aren't seen. Be sure the operator, supervisor, and inspector all understand what they are seeing.

- Be an active investigator. Try changing things that aren't supposed to make any difference and use the control chart to tell you if a difference actually exists.

P charts for proportion defective

Definition   *P charts* are statistical tools used to evaluate the proportion defective produced by a process.

Usage   *P charts* can be applied to any variable where the appropriate performance measure is a unit count. Examples include yield reports, scrap reports, inspection data, and any other data where you know how many units were inspected and how many either met some criteria or failed to meet the criteria. p charts answer the question "Has a special cause of variation caused this process to produce an abnormally large or small number of defective units over the time period observed?" Unlike np charts, p charts can be used when the subgroup size varies. As with np charts, these charts require that the performance measure be *unit counts,* if you are counting the number of occurrences themselves you should use u charts or c charts instead. For example, you would use a p chart if you counted the number of cans with one or more defects. However, if you wanted to

p Chart Worksheet Instructions

1. If possible, collect information on 20 to 25 subgroups.
2. Record the subgroup sizes in column 2 of figure 10.4b.
3. Record the number defective in each subgroup in column 3 of figure 10.4b.
4. Compute the subgroup proportion defective, p, by dividing column 3 by column 2. Record the result in column 4.
5.. Compute the square root of column 2 and record the result in column 5.
6. Add all of the j subgroup sizes in column 2 and record the result in the box.

$$n = \sum_{i=1}^{j} n_i \quad \longrightarrow \quad \boxed{}$$

7. Add the j subgroup defectives in column 3 and record the result in the box.

$$d = \sum_{i=1}^{j} d_i \quad \longrightarrow \quad \boxed{}$$

8. Complete the remaining calculations as shown below. The result will be a constant, C, that is used in column 6 of figure 10.4b.

$$\bar{p} = \frac{d}{n} \quad \longrightarrow \quad \boxed{}$$

$$\bar{q} = 1 - \bar{p} \quad \longrightarrow \quad \boxed{}$$

$$A = \bar{p} \times \bar{q} \quad \longrightarrow \quad \boxed{}$$

$$B = \sqrt{A} \quad \longrightarrow \quad \boxed{}$$

$$C = 3 \times B \quad \longrightarrow \quad \boxed{} \quad \text{Use in column 6 of figure 10.4b}$$

Figure 10.4a-p Chart Worksheet, Part I

Col. 1	Col. 2	Col. 3	Col. 4	Col. 5	Col. 6	Col. 7	Col. 8
Sub-group #	Sub-group Size, n_i	Sub-group Defectives, d_i	$p =$ $\dfrac{Col.\ 3}{Col.\ 2}$	$\sqrt{n_i}$	$\dfrac{C}{Col.\ 5}$	LCL = $\bar{p} - (6)$ or 0	UCL = $\bar{p} + (6)$ or 1
1							
2							
3							
4							
5							
6							
7							
8							
9							
10							
11							
12							
13							
14							
15							
16							
17							
18							
19							
20							
21							
22							
23							
24							
25							
TOTAL							

Figure 10.4b-p Chart Worksheet, Part II

count the defects instead of the cans that had defects you would use a u chart or a c chart. U charts and c charts are described later in this chapter.

How to prepare and analyze p charts

1. Determine the subgroup size, rational subgroup, and sampling frequency. When using p charts the subgroup size can vary. Sampling should be frequent enough to detect the effect of special causes while the special cause itself can still be identified. This varies a great deal from process to process, but as a crude rule of thumb you should average about 1 out of control point per typical control chart of 25 groups. If you have more than that, increase the sampling frequency. If you have fewer, reduce the sampling frequency.
2. Collect data from 20-25 subgroups. While the data is being collected, you should minimize disturbances to the process. If a process change is unavoidable, develop a system for recording changes so that their effect can be determined.
3. Establish the control limits. Perform the necessary calculations. The worksheets in figures 10.4a and 10.4b provide a guide for doing the calculations. There are two parts to the worksheet. The first part computes values that remain fixed for each subgroup, regardless of the subgroup size. The second part consists of subgroup data. By stepping through the worksheet instructions you will calculate control limits for each subgroup on the p chart. The control limits will change as the subgroup sizes change. When the control chart is plotted, the control limits will move in and out as the subgroup sizes vary.
   The equations being solved with the worksheet are

$$\bar{p} = \frac{total\ number\ defective}{total\ number\ inspected} \qquad \text{(10.1 repeated)}$$

$$\text{(10.6)}$$
$$LCL_p = \bar{p} - 3 \sqrt{\frac{\bar{p}(1-\bar{p})}{n_i}}$$

$$\text{(10.7)}$$
$$UCL_p = \bar{p} + 3 \sqrt{\frac{\bar{p}(1-\bar{p})}{n_i}}$$

where n_i is the subgroup size, which may vary from group to group. If LCL < 0 it is set to 0, if UCL > 1 it is set to 1. The numbers actually plotted are the sample values computed and recorded in column 4 of the worksheet.

4. Analysis of p charts. As with all control charts, a special cause is probably present if there are any points beyond either the lower control limit or the upper control limit. Analysis of p chart patterns between the control limits is complicated by two facts: (1) the distribution of the number defective follows the binomial distribution, not the normal dis-

Table 10.3-p Chart Example Data

Shipment No.	# crates checked	# peaches	# bruised
1	1	250	47
2	1	250	42
3	1	250	55
4	1	250	51
5	1	250	46
6	1	250	61
7	1	250	39
8	1	250	44
9	1	250	41
10	1	250	51
11	2	500	88
12	2	500	101
13	2	500	101
14	1	250	40
15	1	250	48
16	1	250	47
17	1	250	50
18	1	250	48
19	1	250	57
20	1	250	45
21	1	250	43
22	2	500	105
23	2	500	98
24	2	500	100
25	2	500	96

p Chart Worksheet Instructions

1. If possible, collect information on 20 to 25 subgroups.
2. Record the subgroup sizes in column 2 of figure 10.4b.
3. Record the number defective in each subgroup in column 3 of figure 10.5b.
4. Compute the subgroup proportion defective, p, by dividing column 3 by column 2. Record the result in column 4.
5.. Compute the square root of column 2 and record the result in column 5.
6. Add all of the j subgroup sizes in column 2 and record the result in the box.

$$n = \sum_{i=1}^{j} n_i \quad \longrightarrow \quad \boxed{8{,}000}$$

7. Add the j subgroup defectives in column 3 and record the result in the box.

$$d = \sum_{i=1}^{j} d_i \quad \longrightarrow \quad \boxed{1{,}544}$$

8. Complete the remaining calculations as shown below. The result will be a constant, C, that is used in column 6 of figure 10.5b.

$$\bar{p} = \frac{d}{n} \quad \longrightarrow \quad \boxed{0.193}$$

$$\bar{q} = 1 - \bar{p} \quad \longrightarrow \quad \boxed{0.807}$$

$$A = \bar{p} \times \bar{q} \quad \longrightarrow \quad \boxed{0.155751}$$

$$B = \sqrt{A} \quad \longrightarrow \quad \boxed{0.39465}$$

$$C = 3 \times B \quad \longrightarrow \quad \boxed{1.1840} \quad \text{Use in column 6 of figure 10.5b}$$

Figure 10.5a-Completed p Chart Worksheet, Part I

Col. 1	Col. 2	Col. 3	Col. 4	Col. 5	Col. 6	Col. 7	Col. 8
Sub-group #	Sub-group Size, n_i	Sub-group Defectives, d_i	p = $\frac{Col.\,3}{Col.\,2}$	$\sqrt{n_i}$	$\frac{C}{Col.\,5}$	LCL = $\bar{p} - (6)$ or 0	UCL = $\bar{p} + (6)$ or 1
1	250	47	0.188	15.8114	0.07488	0.1181	0.2679
2		42	0.168				
3		55	0.220				
4		51	0.204				
5		46	0.184				
6		61	0.244				
7		39	0.156				
8		44	0.176				
9		41	0.164				
10		51	0.204				
11	500	88	0.176	22.3607	0.05295	0.1400	0.2460
12		101	0.202				
13		101	0.202				
14	250	40	0.160	15.8114	0.07488	0.1181	0.2679
15		48	0.192				
16		47	0.188				
17		50	0.200				
18		48	0.192				
19		57	0.228				
20		45	0.180				
21		43	0.172				
22	500	105	0.210	22.3607	0.05295	0.1400	0.2679
23		98	0.196				
24		100	0.200				
25		96	0.192				
TOTAL	8,000	1,544					

Figure 10.5b-Completed p Chart Worksheet, Part II

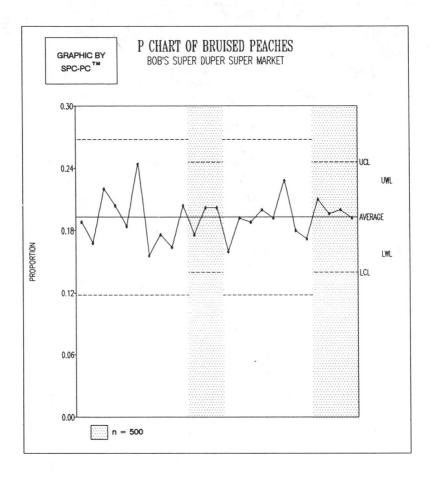

Figure 10.6-Completed p Chart

tribution and (2) the control limits will change as the subgroup sizes change. Because of this, run tests are not usually applied to p charts.

p chart example

Bob, our friendly neighborhood produce manager, has kept track of the number of bruised peaches in recent shipments. The data in table 10.3 were obtained by opening randomly selected crates from each shipment and counting the number of bruised peaches. There are 250 peaches per crate. Normally Bob only samples one crate per shipment. However, when his part-time helper is available Bob samples 2 crates. Since this means the sample size varies a p chart must be used instead of an np chart.

The data in table 10.3 are used to complete the worksheets in figure 10.4. The completed worksheet is shown in figure 10.5 and the completed p chart is shown in figure 10.6.

Related techniques

P charts are used for process control of the number defective when sample size varies. Np control charts are used when the sample size is constant. If the control measure is the number of **defects** instead of the number of defectives (a defective is a **unit** with one or more defects), then a c chart or a u chart is used.

Pointers for using p charts

- If you have a choice, use careful judgement to determine the sample size. For instance, with our example the produce manager used crates.

- Keep a detailed log of the conditions that created a particular subgroup. What vendor's materials were used? Who was the operator? The inspector? etc. Use the information to investigate patterns; are all of the peak defective counts coming from the same vendor or operator?

- Keep the chart near the operation being charted. Control charts are feedback mechanisms that can't work if they aren't seen. Be sure the operator, supervisor, and inspector all understand what they are seeing.

- Be an active investigator. Try changing things that aren't supposed to make any difference and use the control chart to tell you if a difference actually exists.

- Determine if "moving control limits" are really necessary. It may be possible to use the average sample size as defined by equation 10.8. Table 10.4 illustrates the different control limits resulting from 250

Table 10.4-Demonstration of Using Average Sample Size

Sample Size	LCL	UCL
250	0.1181	0.2679
500	0.1400	0.2460
$\bar{n} = \dfrac{8,000}{25} = 320$	0.1268	0.2592

peach subgroups, 500 peach subgroups, and the average sample size, $\bar{n}$, of 320 peaches.

$$\bar{n} = \frac{total\ of\ subgroup\ counts}{number\ of\ subgroups} \tag{10.8}$$

- Notice that the conclusions are the same when using the average sample size as they are using the exact sample sizes. In other words, all subgroup p values are still within the $\bar{n}$ based control limits. This is usually the case if the variation in sample size isn't too great. There are many rules of thumb, but most of them are extremely conservative. The best way is to check it out the way we did here, using real process data. If the conclusions are nearly always the same with exact limits and with $\bar{n}$ based control limits, you can safely go with the $\bar{n}$ based control limits.

C charts for number of occurrences

Definition   *C charts* are statistical tools used to evaluate the number of occurrences produced by a process. Usually an "occurrence" is a defect. This chart is different from an np chart in that we are counting all of the defects; if a unit has more than 1 defect we will count each defect separately. With np charts we count only **defective units**, and a defective unit may contain several defects.

Usage   *C charts* can be applied to any variable where the *sample size is constant* and the appropriate performance measure is a count of some event or class of events. C charts answer the question "Has a special cause of variation caused this process to produce an abnormally large or small number of occurrences over the time period observed?" In usual quality control applications this question is "Has a special cause of variation caused this process to produce an abnormally large or small number of **defects** over the time period observed?"

How to prepare and analyze c charts

1. Determine the subgroup size, rational unit, and sampling frequency. The subgroup size **must be constant for all subgroups** and should be large enough that the chart of number of defective in the sample produces a pattern that can be analyzed. A crude rule of thumb is that the average number of occurrences per unit should be 5 or more. The average number of occurrences per unit is found by

$$\bar{c} = \frac{number\ of\ occurrences}{number\ of\ units\ inspected} \qquad (10.9)$$

Using this rule the unit size would be

$$unit\ size \geq \frac{5}{\bar{c}} \qquad (10.10)$$

In other words, the sample unit size would be selected so that the average number of occurrences per unit was 5 or more. For example, if sampling radar sets and there was an average of 1 defect per set, the unit used for control charting purposes would be 5 radar sets, i.e., 5 radar sets = 1 unit. If you checked 20 subgroups of 5 radar sets each and found 100 defects, you would find the average number of defects per unit using equation 10.9 as follows

$$\bar{c} = \frac{100\ defects}{20\ units} = 5\ defects\ per\ unit$$

Sampling should be frequent enough to detect the effect of special causes while the special cause itself can still be identified. This varies a great deal from process to process, but as a crude rule of thumb you should average about 1 out of control point per typical control chart of 25 groups. If you have more than that, increase the sampling frequency. If you have fewer, reduce the sampling frequency.

2. Collect data from 25 subgroups. While the data is being collected, you should minimize disturbances to the process. If a process change is un-avoidable, develop a system for recording changes so that their effect can be determined.

3. Establish the control limits. Perform the necessary calculations. The flow chart in figure 10.7 provides a guide for doing the calculations.[2] Each arithmetic instruction in the flowchart's computational sequence is accompanied by rectangles divided into three segments: (1) an iden-tification number, (2) a description of the data element or instruction, and (3) a blank space for recording the resultant data. Numbers written beneath the description or instruction in segment (2) refer you back to the rectangles corresponding. In the descriptive portion of rectangle

---

2   Adapted from a flow chart printed in the ASQC Statistics Division Newsletter, June 1986.

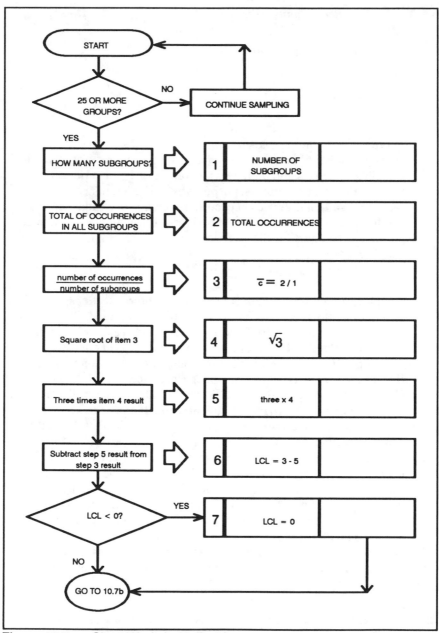

Figure 10.7a-c Chart Worksheet, Part I

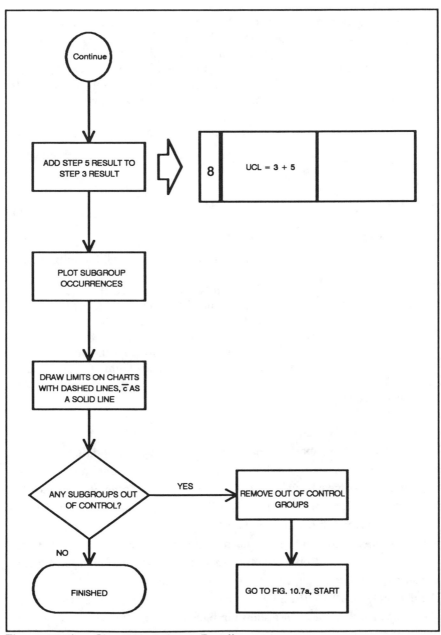

Figure 10.7b-c Chart Worksheet, Part II

number 3 for example, **2/1** means that you should divide the data element written in rectangle number 2 by the data element in rectangle number 1. By stepping through this simple logic, you will calculate control limits for the c chart by the time you complete the worksheet. To distinguish values from rectangle numbers, when we want you to actually use a numeric value, we will spell out the values we want you to use e.g., three x four = twelve.

The equations being solved with the flowchart are

$$\bar{c} = \frac{total\ number\ of\ occurrences}{number\ of\ units} \qquad \text{(10.9 repeated)}$$

$$LCL_c = \bar{c} - 3\sqrt{\bar{c}} \qquad \text{(10.11)}$$

$$UCL_c = \bar{c} + 3\sqrt{\bar{c}} \qquad \text{(10.12)}$$

where $\bar{c}$ is computed as shown in equation 10.9 using all the subgroups combined.

4. Analysis of c charts. As with all control charts, a special cause is probably present if there are any points beyond either the lower control limit or the upper control limit. Analysis of c chart patterns between the control limits is complicated by the fact that the distribution of the number defective follows the Poisson distribution, not the normal distribution. However, if there is both a lower control limit and an upper control limit the pattern is usually close enough to normal to apply the run tests described for $\bar{x}$ charts in chapter 8.

c chart example

Bob, our friendly neighborhood produce manager, has learned that peaches have more problems than merely being bruised. Some peaches are damaged by insects, others have been infected by peach canker. Some peaches have more than one problem. Because of this Bob has decided to actually count the *all flaws* instead of just counting the peaches that have one or more problems. Also, Bob will be sampling a single crate selected at random from each shipment. Since Bob is counting *occurrences* instead of units, and since his sample size is constant, a c chart should be used.

The data in table 10.5 are used to complete the worksheets from figure 10.7. The completed worksheets are shown in figure 10.8 and the completed c control chart is shown in figure 10.9.

Table 10.5-Raw Data for c Chart

Shipment Number	Total Flaws
1	27
2	32
3	24
4	31
5	42
6	38
7	33
8	35
9	35
10	39
11	41
12	29
13	34
14	34
15	43
16	29
17	33
18	33
19	38
20	32
21	37
22	30
23	31
24	32
25	42
26	40
27	21
28	23
29	39
30	29

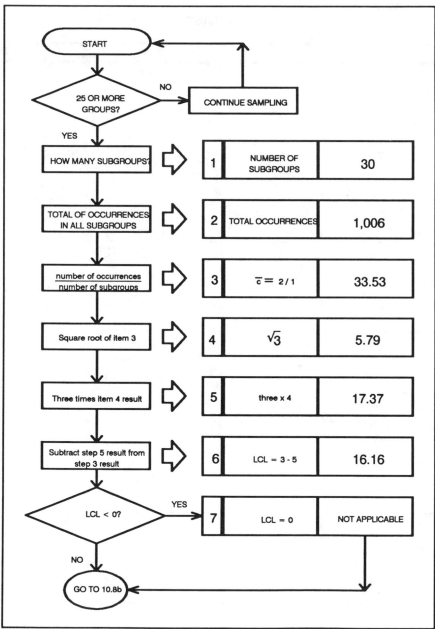

Figure 10.8a-c Chart Worksheet, Part I

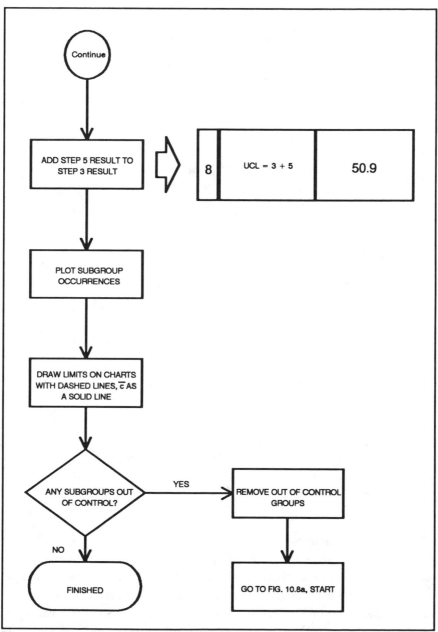

Figure 10.8b-c Chart Worksheet, Part II

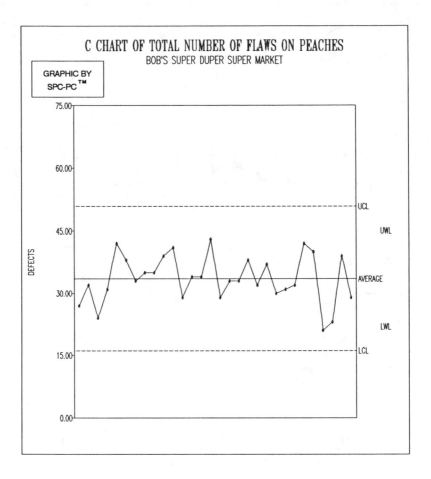

Figure 10.9-Completed c Chart

Related techniques

C control charts are used for process control of the number of occurrences when the sample size is constant. U control charts are used when the sample size varies. If the control measure is the number of **defectives or units** instead of the number of defects or occurrences (a defective is a **unit** with one or more defects), then an np chart or a p chart is used.

138

Pointers for using c charts

● Use careful judgement to determine the sample size and the subgroup. For instance, with our example the produce manager used a crate as the subgroup - quite logical. Peaches within a single crate should be relatively homogenous. The subgroup may be 50 consecutive units sampled at a randomly selected time of day, or a full box, or a full pallet.

● Keep a detailed log of the conditions that created a particular subgroup. Which vendor's materials were used? Who was the operator? The inspector? Use the information to investigate patterns, are all of the peak defective counts coming from the same vendor or operator?

● Keep the chart near the operation being charted. Control charts are feedback mechanisms that can't work if they aren't seen. Be sure the operator, supervisor, and inspector all understand what they are seeing.

● Be an active investigator. Try changing things that aren't supposed to make any difference and use the control chart to tell you if a difference actually exists.

u charts for occurrences per unit

Definition   *U charts* are statistical tools used to evaluate the number of occurrences per unit produced by a process.

Usage   *U charts* can be applied to any variable where the appropriate performance measure is a count of occurrences. In traditional SPC work, the occurrence being counted is a defect, however, many other types of occurrence measures are possible. Examples include solder flaws per 100 solder joints, errors per 100 purchase orders issued, program bugs per 1,000 lines of source code, and any other data where you know how many units were inspected and how many either met some criteria or failed to meet the criteria. U charts answer the question "Has a special cause of variation caused this process to produce an abnormally large or small number of defective units over the time period observed?" Unlike c charts, u charts can be used when the subgroup size varies. As with c charts, these charts require that the performance measure be *occurrence counts,* if you are counting the number of units themselves you should use p charts or np charts instead. For example, you would use a u chart if you counted the number of defects per sample of cans. However, if you wanted to count the number of cans that had one or more defects, instead of the defects themselves, you would use a p

u Chart Worksheet Instructions

1. If possible, collect information on 20 to 25 subgroups.
2. Record the subgroup sizes in column 2 of figure 10.10b.
3. Record the number of occurrences in each subgroup in column 3 of figure 10.10b.
4. Compute the subgroup occurrences per unit by dividing column 3 by column 2. Record the result in column 4.
5.. Compute the square root of column 2 and record the result in column 5.
6. Add all of the j subgroup sizes in column 2 and record the result in the box.

$$n = \sum_{i=1}^{j} n_i \longrightarrow \boxed{}$$

7. Add the j subgroup defectives in column 3 and record the result in the box.

$$o = \sum_{i=1}^{j} o_i \longrightarrow \boxed{}$$

8. Complete the remaining calculations as shown below. The result will be a constant, B, that is used in column 6 of figure 10.10b.

$$\bar{u} = \frac{o}{n} \longrightarrow \boxed{}$$

$$A = \sqrt{\bar{u}} \longrightarrow \boxed{}$$

$$B = 3 \times A \longrightarrow \boxed{}$$ Use in column 6 of figure 10.10b

Figure 10.10a-u Chart Worksheet, Part I

Col. 1	Col. 2	Col. 3	Col. 4	Col. 5	Col. 6	Col. 7	Col. 8
Sub-group #	Size, n_i	Occur-rences, o_i	$u = \dfrac{Col.\,3}{Col.\,2}$	$\sqrt{n_i}$	$\dfrac{B}{Col.\,5}$	LCL = $\bar{u} - (6)$ or 0	UCL = $\bar{u} + (6)$
1							
2							
3							
4							
5							
6							
7							
8							
9							
10							
11							
12							
13							
14							
15							
16							
17							
18							
19							
20							
21							
22							
23							
24							
25							
26							
27							
28							
29							
30							
TOTAL							

Figure 10.10b-u Chart Worksheet, Part II

chart or an np chart. p charts and np charts were described earlier in this chapter.

How to prepare and analyze u charts

1. Determine the subgroup size, rational subgroup, and sampling frequency. When using u charts the subgroup size can vary. Sampling should be frequent enough to detect the effect of special causes while the special cause itself can still be identified. This varies a great deal from process to process, but as a crude rule of thumb you should average about 1 out of control point per 25 groups. If you have more than that, increase the sampling frequency. If you have fewer, reduce the sampling frequency.
2. Collect data from 25 subgroups. While the data is being collected, you should minimize disturbances to the process. If a process change is unavoidable, develop a system for recording changes so that their effect can be determined.
3. Establish the control limits. Perform the necessary calculations. The worksheets in figures 10.10a and 10.10b provide a guide for doing the calculations. There are two parts to the worksheet. The first part computes values that remain fixed for each subgroup, regardless of the subgroup size. The second part consists of subgroup data. By stepping through the worksheet instructions you will calculate control limits for each subgroup on the u chart. The control limits will change if the subgroup sizes change. When the control chart is plotted, the control limits will move in and out as the subgroup sizes vary.

The equations being solved with the worksheet are

$$\bar{u} = \frac{\textit{total number of occurrences}}{\textit{total number of units inspected}} \tag{10.13}$$

$$LCL_u = \bar{u} - 3\sqrt{\frac{\bar{u}}{n_i}} \tag{10.14}$$

$$UCL_u = \bar{u} + 3\sqrt{\frac{\bar{u}}{n_i}} \tag{10.15}$$

where n_i is the subgroup size, which may vary from one subgroup to another. If LCL < 0 it is set to 0. The number actually plotted for each subgroup is in column 4, u. U is computed as

$$u = \frac{subgroup\ occurrences}{number\ of\ units\ in\ subgroup} \qquad (10.16)$$

4. Analysis of u charts. As with all control charts, a special cause is probably present if there are any points beyond either the lower control limit or the upper control limit. Analysis of u chart patterns between the control limits is complicated by two facts: (1) the distribution of the number defective follows the Poisson distribution, not the normal dis-

Table 10.6-u Chart Example Data

Shipment No.	# crates checked	# peaches	# of flaws
1	1	250	47
2	1	250	42
3	1	250	55
4	1	250	51
5	1	250	46
6	1	250	61
7	1	250	39
8	1	250	44
9	1	250	41
10	1	250	51
11	2	500	88
12	2	500	101
13	2	500	101
14	1	250	40
15	1	250	48
16	1	250	47
17	1	250	50
18	1	250	48
19	1	250	57
20	1	250	45
21	1	250	43
22	2	500	105
23	2	500	98
24	2	500	100
25	2	500	96

u Chart Worksheet Instructions

1. If possible, collect information on 20 to 25 subgroups.
2. Record the subgroup sizes in column 2 of figure 10.11b.
3. Record the number of occurrences in each subgroup in column 3 of figure 10.11b.
4. Compute the subgroup occurrences per unit by dividing column 3 by column 2. Record the result in column 4.
5.. Compute the square root of column 2 and record the result in column 5.
6. Add all of the j subgroup sizes (in units) in column 2 and record the result in the box.

$$n = \sum_{i=1}^{j} n_i \longrightarrow \boxed{32}$$

7. Add the j subgroup defectives in column 3 and record the result in the box.

$$o = \sum_{i=1}^{j} o_i \longrightarrow \boxed{1,544}$$

8. Complete the remaining calculations as shown below. The result will be a constant, B, that is used in column 6 of figure 10.10b.

$$\bar{u} = \frac{o}{n} \longrightarrow \boxed{48.25}$$

$$A = \sqrt{\bar{u}} \longrightarrow \boxed{6.9462}$$

$$B = 3 \times A \longrightarrow \boxed{20.839} \quad \text{Use in column 6 of figure 10.10b}$$

Figure 10.11a-Completed u Chart Worksheet, Part I

Col. 1	Col. 2	Col. 3	Col. 4	Col. 5	Col. 6	Col. 7	Col. 8
Sub-group #	Size, n_i (units)	Occur-rences, o_i	$u_i = \dfrac{Col.\,3}{Col.\,2}$	$\sqrt{n_i}$	$\dfrac{B}{Col.\,5}$	LCL = $\bar{u} - (6)$ or 0	UCL = $\bar{u} + (6)$
1	1	47	47	1	20.839	27.411	69.089
2		42	42				
3		55	55				
4		51	51				
5		46	46				
6		61	61				
7		39	39				
8		44	44				
9		41	41				
10		51	51				
11	2	88	44	1.4142	14.736	33.514	62.986
12		101	50.5				
13		101	50.5				
14	1	40	40	1	20.839	27.411	69.089
15		48	48				
16		47	47				
17		50	50				
18		48	48				
19		57	57				
20		45	45				
21		43	43				
22	2	105	52.5	1.4142	14.736	33.514	62.986
23		98	49				
24		100	50				
25		96	48				
26							
27							
28							
29							
30							
TOTAL	32	1,544					

Figure 10.11b-Completed u Chart Worksheet, Part II

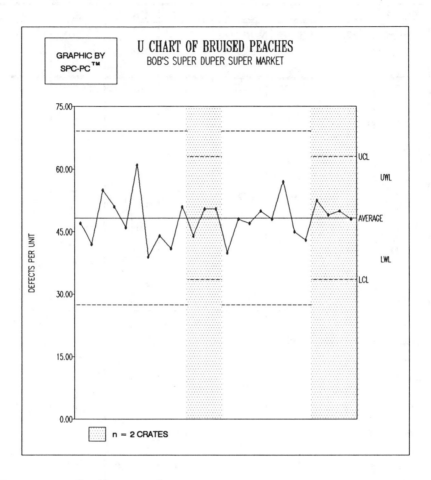

Figure 10.12-Completed u Chart

tribution and (2) the control limits will change as the subgroup sizes change. Because of this, run tests are not usually applied to u charts.

u chart example

Bob, our friendly neighborhood produce manager, has kept track of the number of "flawed" peaches in recent shipments. The data in table 10.6 were obtained by opening randomly selected crates from each shipment and counting the number of flaws on all peaches. A unit is defined as one crate. Normally Bob only samples one crate per shipment. However, when his part-time helper is available Bob samples 2 crates. Since this means the sample size varies, a u chart must be used instead of a c chart.

The data in table 10.6 are used to complete the worksheets in figure 10.10. The completed worksheet is shown in figure 10.11 and the completed p control chart is shown in figure 10.12.

Related techniques

U charts are used for process control of the number of occurrences when sample size varies. C charts are used when the sample size is constant. If the control measure is the number of **defectives** instead of the number of occurrences (a defective is a **unit** with one or more defects), then an np chart or a p chart is used.

Pointers for using u charts

- If you have a choice, use careful judgement to determine the sample size. For instance, with our example the produce manager used crates as the subgroup - quite logical. The subgroup may be 50 consecutive units sampled at a randomly selected time of day, or a full box, or a full pallet.

Table 10.7-Demonstration of Using Average Sample Size

Sample Size	LCL	UCL
1 unit (crate)	27.411	69.089
2 units	33.514	62.986
$\bar{n} = \dfrac{32}{25} = 1.28\,units$	29.831	66.67

- Keep a detailed log of the conditions that created a particular subgroup. What vendor's materials were used? Who was the operator? The inspector? etc. Use the information to investigate patterns; are all of the peak defective counts coming from the same vendor or operator?

- Keep the chart near the operation being charted. Control charts are feedback mechanisms that can't work if they aren't seen. Be sure the operator, supervisor, and inspector all understand what they are seeing.

- Be an active investigator. Try changing things that aren't supposed to make any difference and use the control chart to tell you if a difference actually exists.

- Determine if "moving control limits" are really necessary. It may be possible to use the average sample size as defined by equation 10.17. Table 10.7 illustrates the different control limits resulting from 1 unit subgroups, 2 unit subgroups, and the average sample size, $\bar{n}$, of 1.28 units.

$$\bar{n} = \frac{total\ number\ of\ units}{number\ of\ subgroups} \qquad (10.17)$$

- Notice that the conclusions are the same when using the average sample size as they are using the exact sample sizes. In other words, all subgroup u values are still within the $\bar{n}$ based control limits. This is usually the case if the variation in sample size isn't too great. There are many rules of thumb, but most of them are extremely conservative. The best way is to check it out the way we did here, using real process data. If the conclusions are nearly always the same with exact limits and with $\bar{n}$ based control limits, you can safely go with the $\bar{n}$ based control limits.

Index of Volume One

A

B

C

Fukuda, Ryuji 36

G

H

I

J

M

N